SELECTED POEMS OF

P. B. SHELLEY

D0774579

THE POETRY BOOKSHELF

General Editor: James Reeves

SELECTED POEMS OF

PERCY BYSSHE SHELLEY

*Edited with an Introduction
and Notes
by*

JOHN HOLLOWAY

HEINEMANN
LONDON

Heinemann Educational Books Ltd
22 Bedford Square, London WC1B 3HH

LONDON EDINBURGH MELBOURNE AUCKLAND
HONG KONG SINGAPORE KUALA LUMPUR NEW DELHI
IBADAN NAIROBI JOHANNESBURG KINGSTON
EXETER (NH) PORT OF SPAIN

ISBN 0 435 15027 8

P. B. SHELLEY 1792–1822

INTRODUCTION AND NOTES © JOHN HOLLOWAY 1960
FIRST PUBLISHED 1960
REPRINTED 1964, 1965, 1967, 1969, 1973, 1977,
1979

Printed and bound in Great Britain by
Morrison & Gibb Ltd, London and Edinburgh

CONTENTS

Appendix A: Verse Translations by Shelley

Appendix B: Extracts from Shelley's translation of Plato's Symposium:

PREFACE

THE *Introduction* which follows this Preface discusses Shelley's poetry, and a summary of his life and development is to be found in the subsequent *Summary*. The *Selections* are arranged, without formal divisions, in a sequence of: poems with a clear auto-biographical interest; political and satirical poems; lyrics; odes and elegies; and finally, narrative poems or extracts from *Prometheus Unbound*. The dates of composition, unless they have already been given in the *Summary*, appear in the *Notes*. The poems, especially the short poems regularly divided into stanzas, have been printed with a minimum of line numbering and other distractions. The *Appendices* contain two of Shelley's verse translations, followed by two key passages from his translation of Plato's *Symposium*; the latter have been included both for their intrinsic interest, and for the light they shed on several of Shelley's more important original works, especially *The Witch of Atlas* and *The Triumph of Life*.

I am indebted, and record thanks, to the General Editor of the series, to Mr. J. B. Bamborough, and to Dr. D. A. Davie.

J. H.

QUEENS' COLLEGE, CAMBRIDGE

INTRODUCTION

THE POETRY OF SHELLEY

COLERIDGE in Malta, Wordsworth in the Alps, Scott cruising
in the Mediterranean—it is not here that we turn for the central
facts about these writers and their work. There were two con-
trasting generations of authors in the 'Romantic Movement
in Britain; and one must start from that, in order to comprehend
Shelley's place. The inspiration of the earlier group was in
essence traditional and local; or if as in the case of Coleridge it
was not strictly local, it certainly belonged to the North of
Europe. The radical principles, the enthusiasm, the idealism of
the French Revolution, were facts that it was part of their
development to set aside, to see beyond. Byron, Shelley, and
Keats had other facts, neither less nor more true, to learn: that
if to oust the *ancien régime* led only to the Terror and Napoleon,
to oust Napoleon led only to Metternich, Lord Liverpool, and
the 'Holy' Alliance. 'The beggars have changed places, but the
lash goes on', wrote Yeats. Shelley points to the contemporary
realities in his sonnet, 'Feelings of a Republican on the Fall of
Bonaparte',

> I know
> Too late, since thou and France are in the dust,
> That Virtue owns a more eternal foe
> Than Force or Fraud: old Custom, legal Crime,
> And bloody Faith the foulest birth of Time.

England after 1815, however, was no place for republicans.
Shelley, Byron, and Keats, all radicals to a greater or lesser
degree, stood in a small minority, the object on political grounds

of active dislike and bitter attack. With them, in fact, comes the first appearance in Britain of the poet as something of an outcast from conventional society and (in sharp contrast to, say, 'bohemian' eighteenth-century poets like Savage or Smart) something of, by conscious choice, an enemy to it.

This second generation of Romantic poets also had quite different cultural affiliations from those who came just before them. Partly again, this is a reflection of politics. Lord Byron, just entered into his inheritance, was unable to go on the conventional Grand Tour because the war with Napoleon was at its height: consequently, he made a much more ambitious and exotic visit by sea to the Mediterranean (1809–10), and took in Spain, Sicily, and Turkey, which the conventional journey of earlier times would by no means have done. Shelley's dash south with Mary Godwin in 1814 may have been partly through a desire to see the land of Rousseau only a few months after the way to it had been reopened, following many years of total closure, by the defeat of Napoleon. Yet these are probably not the vital facts. One of the greatest cultural discoveries of the eighteenth century was what might be called the romanticism of southern Europe specifically as classical Europe and the Classical world—Greece above all. The excavation of Greek Pompeii, the discovery of Baalbec and Palmyra by Robert Wood, the growing fame of the Greek temples at Paestum, the cult of Greek vases, the bringing of the Elgin Marbles to London in 1812, the growing interest in Neo-Platonism chiefly through the work of Thomas Taylor, are all facts which enter the work either of one or other of these three poets themselves, or of writers like Peacock who personally influenced them. For the world which kindled their imagination they turned not north but to the Mediterranean.

Keats is not in the same case as Byron and Shelley. Enthusiastic for the Greeks and their mythology he may have been, but a taste for the landscape of contemporary southern Europe would have been beyond his means, and it must be remembered that he looked back to the world of the northern ballads for some of his best work, and that for him Shakespeare was always an immensely important native influence as he was not for the others. But the exotic quality in both the lives and the work of Byron and Shelley is essentially connected with the bond that held them to the south. Besides everything else, both were deeply influenced by Italian literature. Shelley was also influenced by Spanish drama, and in particular was the first English poet, at least since Chaucer, who proved himself able to draw upon Dante and to naturalize Dante's kind of poetry in English.

Shelley's career, certainly, was exotic and colourful enough. He was nearly expelled from Eton for rebellion. He was expelled from Oxford for something like professing atheism. He made a runaway Scottish marriage with an obscure but beautiful girl. He agitated for a Republic of Ireland at the very moment of the triumph of the Concert of Europe against France. At one time a professed opponent, on principle, of marriage, he eloped with Godwin's daughter (herself a gifted literary woman) to Switzerland. His first wife committed suicide. He was deprived of the custody of his children by the verdict of the Lord Chancellor. He quarrelled intermittently with his father, who sought to have him relinquish his right to the Shelley estates. He became a restless immigrant in Italy, an associate of the then notorious Lord Byron, and a reckless if competent sailor. His poetry drew on at least five foreign languages, his thought ranged from Tom Paine to Plato, he dabbled in Arabic. Finally, his ship foundered in a squall off perhaps the most picturesque stretch of the whole Italian coast, his body was washed ashore and (as the law required) buried in quicklime; later it was exhumed and ceremoniously burned on a funeral pyre on the beach. His ashes, all except the heart, were taken to Rome for their final interment; but the heart, we are told, was inconsumable.

To all this must be added the enigmas of Shelley's personality, with its combination of insight and innocence, of quick sympathy for others and something like self-absorption, and the enigma of his reputation, which has ranged (with about equal degrees of fatuity) from that of an unprincipled monster to that of a poetic saint. All in all, it is easy to see him, when his life and his work are both taken into account, as the most extraordinary and colourful of all English poets. Shelley as a life and a legend, has become, to some one of the great treasures, to others one of the great embarrassments, of our literary history.

II

I would sooner take away from the mass of work done on Shelley's life than add to it. This short book has no speculations to offer about the episodes in Shelley's life which some writers have been most eager to attack, defend, or pry out. The biographical summary which follows lays the stress only upon events in his inner or outer life which seem to be significant in his poetic and intellectual development, or (what is part of that) are connected with the writing of his better poems. There is a more important legend about Shelley than the legend about his life. There is a legend about his verse. Literary history is full of confusions which have been bred from the confusions which preceded them. Shelley's present reputation in many circles is an example of this: just as Milton's is another. Milton was once admired for the 'organ-note' of his poetry. When it came, very properly, to be thought that poetry was not made good merely by such notes as that, the diagnosis was left essentially unchanged, the verdict founded on it was reversed. (Yeats's line comes again to mind.) Shelley was once admired for the ethereal beauty, the intangible quintessential music, the haunting unreality of his verse (and personality). These qualities have come to seem trivial in themselves, and to have regard to them has come to seem the hallmark of an exasperating *belle-lettrisme*. The exasperation is indulged, Shelley is condemned, and the fact that, through the critics' hastiness, we have been, in Dryden's phrase, 'cozened by a jelly', and now cozened not once but twice over, remains unnoticed.

There is so much to say of a positive kind about the nature and development of Shelley's poetry, and it would be a pity to use up space rebutting errors and confusions about it which are easily removed by a truly attentive and open-minded reading of his poetry itself. Yet certain preliminary points are worth making. The tabloid version of English poetic history which we owe to T. S. Eliot's early essays ('. . . a dissociation of sensibility set in, from which we have never recovered . . .') seems now to be losing the hold on readers' minds which it once had. In its time it encouraged the idea that in Shelley's poetry the intellect naturally did either no work at all, or only the inappropriate work of supplying a mass of poetically indigestible philosophical or political doctrines. This is a plain error of fact, one which is made plain not so much by noticing the considered and multiple corrections and changes in the manuscripts of Shelley's poems, as from such poems as *An Exhortation* (p. 42) or 'Rarely, rarely, comest thou' (p. 36) or *To Jane*, (p. 40) or, finally, the *Ode to Heaven* (p. 55). There is no need to look further than these poems, which save for the last are all comparatively simple, to recognize how Shelley's intelligence could operate not as that of a philosopher in his verse, but essentially as that of a poet, thinking and working through the detailed fabric of the verse, controlling and modulating the tone, and creating a train of thought, intricate and exact yet unforced and unostentatious, of which the metre, the rhyming, the stanza, come to form the necessary vehicle.

I point to these poems (some of their details are briefly discussed in the notes) because they bring decisively to notice a Shelley who has been overlooked. Yet the capacity to conduct an argument in poetry is a modest talent, even though it is one which a poet should not be without: and the first two poems mentioned above are modest achievements in that they go little beyond this. Once we have learnt, however, to look in Shelley for qualities of mind which the tabloid acccount of English poetic history encouraged us to assume were absent, a genuinely poetic mental life, controlling and manoeuvring material much more varied than the steps of any argument, and doing so with an intricacy and dexterity which few English poets have equalled, begins to be apparent in much of his work. To many readers this will sound surprising and unplausible; I can only add that it is something which I have had to teach myself, against the current of a now widespread opinion about Shelley, slowly and with difficulty and incredulity. The first semichorus of Spirits from *Prometheus Unbound*, Act II, Scene ii, and the *Ode to the West Wind* are discussed in some detail in the notes from this point of view. Dr. Leavis has severely censured the second of these pieces for (in part) the absence of just such qualities of exact and intelligent organization as I am now attributing to it; but his discussion gives one every reason to suppose that he has simply not recognized, save in a vague and inaccurate way, the realities with which Shelley was dealing. This is a decisive defect, but hardly an unnatural one: part of the difficulty of Shelley's work (the point will be considered again later) is that his facts are often distinctive and, to many modern readers, recondite. When the *Ode* is understood at every point, it is still not a perfect poem, but that it is an extraordinary achievement of the whole mind of a true poet comprehensively at work to unify a great variety of poetic material in its linguistic embodiment, seems to me simple truth. The fact is, that Shelley's poetry is far from easy; often enough it is too difficult for his detractors and his champions both. I believe that the present book makes the underlying ideas and at the same time the detailed local structure of some of his more important poems clear, at least for the general reader, for the first time; but in saying that he is too difficult for his critics I do not except myself, and am quite prepared to discover that there is more in some of his work than I have been able to see, or at least reveal.

III

Probably most readers are less troubled by the supposed defects in Shelley's poetic intelligence than by those in his emotions. As is the case (though in very different ways) with Wordsworth, Shelley has roots deep in the eighteenth century; or rather, in some of the less pedestrian and also less sound sides of that period. We can see this in the resonance and sometimes even stilted formality of his prose; in his early addiction to the 'gothic' novel, an addiction which had its effect not only in his two early (and worthless) prose romances, but also here and there in his later work; and again, in a kind of emotionalism which is reminiscent of the cult of sensibility, the selfconscious tears of Sterne and the rest, and the verse of his early correspondent Felicia Hemans. It is no part of my purpose to defend this strain in Shelley; though, if we are concerned for the moment with what it reveals of the man, we must recall such facts as that he never published many of the poems to which objection may be made along these lines, and that *Stanzas written in Dejection near Naples*, with *Lines written among the Euganean Hills*, followed closely upon the death of his daughter Clara, while the *Ode to the West Wind* stands in a not dissimilar relation to the death of his son William. Besides this, it is clear that Shelley's literary isolation, lack of readers in England, and receipt of little but sustained calumny from many English reviewers, oppressed him deeply throughout his last years. For all that, this part of his poetry remains what it is.

Yet if this train of thought is taken further, it will bring the reader to certain vital facts which must be borne in mind before much of the poetry of this period (not Shelley's alone, but often enough, that of his contemporaries as well) can be accurately assessed. The modern reader, over and over again, is likely to form the impression that Shelley must have had his thoughts and feelings, and hence of necessity his language, only half under control. Felicities and ineptitudes appear to alternate in his work with bewildering abruptness. This is something which his admirers have scarcely faced: often enough they have been those who barely see the problem. But to the reader who is not satisfied until he can sense the poem growing like a living thing from individual word to word,

> Let the tyrants pour around
> With a quick and *startling* sound
> Like the loosening of a sea,
> Troops of armed emblazonry.
> > (*The Mask of Anarchy*, 303-4)

seems like a sudden lapse into lameness.

> Thou young Dawn,
> Turn all thy dew to *splendour*
> > (*Adonais*, 362-3)

seems a typical piece of strained Shelleyan vagueness. When, in the *Hymn to Intellectual Beauty*, Shelley writes,

> Sudden, thy shadow fell on me;
> *I shrieked, and clasped my hands in ecstasy!*

his poem seems to become disastrously embarrassing. When, in *The Sensitive Plant*, we read of

> A *Lady*, the wonder of her kind,
> Whose form was upborne by a *lovely mind*

it is much easier to think that we are confronting the language, and the emotional response, of Wardour Street than of a major poet.

Yet that is an attitude which it is impossible to sustain, even for two lines further:

> a lovely mind
> Which, *dilating, had moulded her mien and motion*
> *Like a sea-flower unfolded beneath the ocean.*

Here after all, if only we could ignore those sudden false notes, like a wolf on a violin, is a genuinely imaginative perception of how the mind of a human being can exalt everything about the body; a perception confirmed in a true poet's metaphor, apt yet remote, and also one intrinsically beautiful. Wardour Street is a world away. What, then, is going on? And do the lines from the *Hymn to Intellectual Beauty* take on another appearance, when they are set beside the closing lines of Keats's *Hyperion*, to which they bear an intriguing resemblance?—

> During the pain Mnemosyne upheld
> Her arms as one who prophesied.—At length
> *Apollo shriek'd;*—and lo! from all his limbs
> Celestial Glory dawn'd; he was a god![1]

The fact is, that the poetry of this period confronts the modern reader with a difficulty which has scarcely been remarked on, although is pervasive and acute. It may be seen as a matter of emotions, responses, and attitudes, or of the vocabulary in which these are expressed. Ideally it should be seen as both of these together. Leading attitudes and feelings of earlier times, often also pervasive in the poetry of those times, have in many cases entirely disappeared from the modern mind. When this happens, the words which gave them expression either become obsolete, or entirely lose the particular sense or associations which they were lent by the obsolete attitude or feeling. Both attitude and meaning are overlooked by the general reader, and are carefully recovered and restored by the scholarly one.

[1] The last line is completed here from the Woodhouse MS.

This would be the case, for example, with the idea of universal hierarchy which (as who does not now know?) was so influential in Shakespeare's time, and with a word like 'relation' which, through this idea, then meant something a good deal richer emotionally than it does to-day.

The special problem with a poet like Shelley is that many of the attitudes, situations, and ideas in his work are such as a modern reader can neither remain unaware of nor recover in a mint state. The isolation of the artist, 'ideal beauty', idealized love between men and women, skylarks singing, the sensations of incipient syncope which appear to be a frequent concomitant, even among the flyest, of extreme physical desire, and the notion of a great social and spiritual regeneration of mankind, are things in quite a different class from cosmic correspondence or universal hierarchy. Nothing is harder than to take them strictly at their face value in a poem. This is so because (whatever critics may have come to prefer) it is the ideas and attitudes and emotions which the Romantic Movement minted that have now penetrated down into every corner of modern life and modern awareness; that have been cheapened everywhere around us; that have descended to ubiquitous banality through a thousand channels. Legitimate burlesque then completes what vulgarization began. It is not a matter of Shelley alone, though he suffers more than the others. Echoes of Wordsworth's 'Immortality Ode' may turn up in a Children's Home appeal, of Keats on the Nightingale or Coleridge on the artist across the sleeve of a long-playing record, of Shelley's 'glorious Phantom' (p. 16) from a Marble Arch stump-orator. There is no need to prolong the dreary catalogue, painful in itself, and doubly so for what it has done to our literature.

As with the feelings and ideas, so of necessity with the language. 'Lovely mind' could once mean something exact and significant. In contemporary English it can only justify a shudder. The newspaper has deprived 'startling' of its original connexion with awakening from sleep, and 'splendour' (useful for coronations and reviews of the Fleet) of its connexion with sparkle and radiance. These are the meanings which transform what Shelley wrote from vague or banal to precise and appropriate: from the occurrence of these words elsewhere in Shelley than the passages quoted above, and also in his contemporaries, it is clear that these are the meanings which they legitimately had for him. Something similar applies very often to the language of the Romantics. Lamb obligingly records perhaps the first stage by which 'awful' became the sort of word which now seems only embarrassing in serious poetry ('she is indeed, *as the Americans express it,* something awful'; 1834, O.E.D.). Business correspondence has presumably transformed the tone of 'the same', an idiom not infrequent in Shelley, Keats, and Browning (I believe that it occurs at least once in Wordsworth) and rendered it poetically preposterous. Words and phrases like 'madness' (poetic rapture), 'green wilderness', and 'maniac' (*Prometheus Unbound,* IV, 470, where it means 'mantic'), also require a certain mental adjustment if they are not to seem to strike false notes. 'Lady' (compare Coleridge's *Dejection Ode*), 'sweet', and 'thrilling' are examples too obvious to need comment.

All this is more than a matter of recourse to the dictionary. Shelley's poetry can usually sustain, but must invariably receive, reading by a mind which is fully and intently in play, a mind from which the world of the film, the cosmetic advertisement and the song hit is for the time being ruthlessly expunged; a mind which can make reference easily (though not slavishly) to Shelley's own leading ideas, and which above all can hear his words with the values which they naturally and genuinely had for him and in his time. To those (there are some) who say that this approach to literature is intrinsically harmful, or that all literature, if it is truly significant, can and must be read as we read the literature of our own age, there is a short answer. In a praiseworthy and (I must concede) urgently justified desire to prevent the sterilization of past literature by toilsome pedantry, they have slipped into an elementary confusion. To read past literature in the real, living, sensitive way they desire, that in which we read the work of our great contemporaries, is not to read it as a barbarian fingers an inscription and takes it for (what he understands) a drawing. It is simply to read it in the way I have tried to describe. This may not be obvious at once: on reflection it will be found, I believe, to become so.

IV

Shelley's work is intimately of its time in more ways than these. Professor Grabo and others have indicated how the science of the period, or at least (as is reasonable) the more or less popular science, enters into his work. Shelley was widely and variously informed about, for example, astronomy and meteorology; and sometimes, a detail picked on by a modern critic for censure on the ground of arbitrariness or confusion has a genuine basis in the scientific opinion of the time. Dr. Davie, for example, condemns Shelley's *Cloud* for saying:

> Sublime on the towers of my skiey bowers
> The lightning my pilot sits.

'There is no reason in natural philosophy to give a basis in logic to the notion that a cloud is directed by electric charges' is his comment.[1] In making it, Dr. Davie was presumably ignorant that this (no doubt erroneous) theory is exactly what Shelley had learnt from his teacher of science, Dr. Adam Walker, who was reputable enough to be employed as a visiting lecturer at Eton, and in whose *Analysis of a Course of Lectures on Experimental Philosophy* we can find other ideas, besides this, like those of Shelley's poem. Not that Shelley's knowledge of science adds much directly to his stature as a poet. Here *Queen Mab* is

[1] *Purity of Diction in English Verse* (1952), p. 135.

instructive. Just as this poem draws on Rousseau, Hume, Godwin, Baron d'Holbach, and Condorcet for its political and religious ideas, and makes of them (as might be expected) something strained and rhetorical, so it draws widely on eighteenth-century cosmic poetry for a kind of buoyant and grandiose cosmic emotion, and its usually didactic, declamatory tone has clear affinities with Akenside's *Pleasures of the Imagination* or Brooke's *Universal Beauty*. To a large extent, it is an eighteenth-century work of a conventional kind.

But one major key to Shelley's development as a poet is, that what begins as mere knowledge of theory becomes in the course of time more intimately a part of his personal experience and response; and the indirect impact of his interest in science on his poetry was great, if it is this which led to the quite special area of experience where (despite legends to the contrary) Shelley as a descriptive poet has a firm and intimate grasp of reality. To an extent, this is true about the reality of ordinary conversation and everyday surroundings. The *Letter to Maria Gisborne* and *The Boat on the Serchio* bring this out clearly, and have been given a prominent position in this selection. It has also seemed worth while to include (in Appendix A) a large part of Shelley's free rendering of the Homeric *Hymn to Mercury*, which is one of his most enjoyable pieces, and shows peculiarly well how wit, liveliness, and everyday realism could fuse with the more imaginative side of his mind. In the end, though, it is this more imaginative side of Shelley which is most remarkable, which is unique; and the point here is that it has a realism of its own.

Shelley, more perhaps than any other poet, possesses an imaginative insight into nature as a world of events and processes, especially those which occur through a great volume of space. His imagination comes to life before the movements of the sun and planets as tangible realities, the transmission of light or sound through the air, the development of things as they grow, the great cycles of interaction between sea, land, and air which are the determinants of climate. It is a gift such as might start with the insight of science, but it has become the insight of a poet or an artist. In the universal cataclysms of the geological past

> the blue globe
> Wrapped deluge round it like a cloak.
> *(Prometheus Unbound,* iv, 314–5)

Spring comes

> Driving sweet buds like flocks to feed on air
> *(Ode to the West Wind,* 11)

an image of which I at least never saw the point, until I watched great flocks of sheep, spreading across a whole landscape, being slowly driven up to their summer mountain pastures. When Shelley makes *The Cloud* say

> I pass through the *pores* of the ocean and shores
> *(The Cloud,* 75)

there seems again, behind the emphatic concrete word, a real sense of the passage of river into the sea and sea into vapour. And here is Shelley's account of how the nightingale sings (it is from *Rosalind and Helen,* written in 1817):

> Daylight on its last purple cloud
> Was lingering grey, and soon her strain
> The nightingale began; now loud,
> Climbing in circles the windless sky,
> Now dying music; suddenly
> 'Tis scattered in a thousand notes,
> And now to the hushed ear it floats
> Like field smells known in infancy,
> Then failing, soothes the air again.

The same concrete awareness is plain: air is a volume, sound spreads in it and through it like a moving thing or a perfume.

(Those who wish to dwell on the fact that smells do not float to the ear are free to do so.) It would be easy, of course, to attack this passage from a position one jump behind the writer, 'Climbing in circles' will seem a fantastic phrase, to those who cannot recall the gradual pealing *crescendo* of the nightingale's song which it so unexpectedly and then so exactly conveys. Something of this kind, perhaps, is widely relevant to criticizing poetry on points of factual detail. The poet is likely—what is often forgotten—to be always right as against the critic. A man who refers in a poem to the nightingale, thereby strongly suggests that he has interested himself in nightingales as well as poems. There is an antecedent likelihood that he will know something of what he writes about. But the critic is in a different position. He in no way criticizes a poem that refers to a nightingale because of any interest in that bird; and the likelihood that he will be even as well informed as the poet, on not one but a variety of subjects which the latter exclusively has chosen, is virtually nil. Nor, very often, can he easily remedy his ignorance, even if he is honest enough to recognize it. All this seems obvious enough; but failure to think these issues out must be behind the arrogance and ineptitude of much that critics have written to correct poets on matters of detail. It is merely a question of who, under the circumstances, may expect to learn from whom. This is very relevant to one of Mr. Eliot's disparagements of Shelley. With regard to the lines:

> The world's great age begins anew
> The golden years return,
> The earth doth like a snake renew
> Her winter weeds outworn:

he writes 'It is not . . . easy to see the propriety of an image which divests a snake of "winter weeds" '. That this critic should be so ignorant of snakes as to think that 'weeds' in this passage means 'plants', is difficult to believe: but I can find no less feeble explanation for his bewildering objection. At such a level, only too often, has been the dismissal of Shelley.

V

This goes to show that the word 'unsubstantial', often enough used of Shelley's verse, is often enough inaccurate. It remains the case that one part of experience was what best kindled his imagination; and that if this was a more significant part than what kindled, say, Tennyson's descriptive powers, it was also, to say the least, less central and immediate in life than the human awareness which is so often present, and present among so much else, in Keats or in Hopkins. All this, however, falls short of the crucial issue. If there were things which Shelley took it upon himself to describe, he had to describe them effectively; but that he was often able to do this is relevant locally, to the memorable phrase or line or passage, rather than to what is most distinctive of his chief works as wholes.

When Shelley's development, at least in the longer poems which are so decisively prominent in what he did, is reviewed in general, a striking fact emerges, and one essentially about his work as poetry, not as something else. A mischievous and misleading way of stating this would be to say, *his poetry becomes less and less about real things*. The early *Queen Mab* admittedly has a scaffolding of fantasy or myth; but in the main it is description, argument, assertion, on matters of science, politics, religion. The other early narrative works (*The Revolt of Islam* and *Rosalind and Helen*, 1817: *Julian and Maddalo*, 1818), are far of course from realist ones; but, however extravagant, they are set in the world itself, they are narratives in a sense not altogether different from that in which Crabbe's poems are narratives. From about 1818, however, something essentially new appears. On the surface, this could be through the influence of Southey's romances like *The Curse of Kehama*. But although it is clear that *Prometheus Unbound* owes something, both in detail and in large outline, to that colourful and ridiculous work, on any serious consideration the two are entirely different in kind. Shelley has by now begun his absorption in Plato; the central hinge of his action seems to draw upon a doctrine of alternating divine entry into the cosmos and alienation from it which Plato advances in his *Statesman*; and the whole work (despite its blemishes) has not that piecemeal kind of deeper meaning for which 'allegory' is the word, but the much more unitary deeper meaning which is pointed to by the word *myth*. *Prometheus Unbound* is a philosophical poem in a predominantly narrative form. *The Mask of Anarchy* (autumn 1819) illustrates the same trend, but much more strikingly. Here Shelley has chosen to pass judgement upon a current political event and the issues which it embodied; and yet, even so, he has worked largely through creating a mythical narrative which depicts the Triumph of Anarchy challenged by a great Satanic angel, and which turns for its figures and situations above all to Spenser and to Milton. The fullest developments of this trend are in *The Witch of Atlas* (1820), *Adonais* (1821), and *The Triumph of Life* (1822; unfinished). All of these, the first to some degree playfully, the others in full seriousness, operate not through any picture of the world as it is (in the plain sense), but through inventing an action which is in essence part of a world into which the detail of the real world enters only tangentially, a world transformed by an imagination that is far from vague only because it is more than realistic.

> Morning sought
> Her eastern watch-tower, and her hair unbound,
> Wet with the tears which should adorn the ground,
> Dimmed the aereal eyes that kindle day

—to think that writing like this may be judged by considering how well it describes a woman in tears is to have no contact with it.

A passage strikingly like the last, but from *The Triumph of Life*, brings out the problems posed by Shelley's later work more fully. The scene is near to one in Dante's *Purgatorio* (this whole poem owes much of its detail and its ideas to Petrarch's *Trionfi*, but it is surely far superior to these poems; its tone and treatment are profoundly Dantesque, and mark indeed the naturalization of that poet into English). Rousseau is describing to the poet himself how, shortly after he was born, he seemed to encounter

> A shape all light, which with one hand did fling
> Dew on the earth, as if she were the dawn, . . .
> In her right hand she bore a crystal glass,
> Mantling with bright Nepenthe: the fierce splendour
> Fell from her as she moved under the mass
> Of the deep cavern, and with palms so tender,
> Their tread broke not the mirror of its billow,
> Glided along the river and did bend her
> Head under the dark boughs, till like a willow
> Her fair hair swept the bosom of the stream
> That whispered with delight to be its pillow.

This is no beautiful picture for its own sake. Platonic philosophy is now providing Shelley not with ideas only, but actually with the fictions through which these may be dramatized. Drawing, probably, on Plotinus (it is very difficult not to believe, as Yeats believed, that the details of this poem, and also of *The Witch of Atlas*, issue from knowledge of Porphyry's essay *On the Cave of the Nymphs*) Shelley is depicting, in narrative form, the Platonic idea of how, in the soul at birth, the memory of a superior ante-natal world is expunged as preparation for the world of sense. The counterpart to this descent from a better to a worse world makes the turning-point of *Adonais*:

> Peace, peace! he is not dead, he doth not sleep—
> He hath awakened from the dream of life—

The spirit of Keats has already gone 'Back to the burning fountain whence it came'.

Some readers may be able to accommodate these ideas by transmuting them into (what, nevertheless, does them violence) Christian terms; or a very few may find them sympathetic or even convincing as they stand. But the majority are likely to be ill at ease, and to wonder whether Shelley has not turned his back on life, to amuse himself (but not them) with airy and meaningless fables. This is a superficial view; and it is worth while suggesting a way in which these later poems may be recognized as not a repudiation, but an extension and perhaps even a deepening, of the reformist enthusiasm which dominates the earlier ones. Plato's idealism, as a philosophical doctrine, went not with unrealistic dreaming but with a sombre and unflinching awareness of the savage realities which are integral to (though not the whole of) the public world. For confirmation of this one need look no further than the metaphor of the ship in a storm (*Republic*, 488) or the account of the stages whereby the good state becomes evil (Books VIII–IX). Pictures like these, and Plato's account of the evil and indeed also the unhappiness of the tyrant, easily enough took up what Shelley had already acquired from eighteenth-century radical thought. All in all, the transition which he made from Godwin to Plato was quite logical and imaginatively coherent. Perhaps the sharpest change, indeed, was one that personal experience and the current state of Europe were both teaching Shelley, at the same time as Plato was suggesting it: that to bring about the millenium is an almost hopeless dream, and moreover that if the millenium were to be realized it would probably prove transient. To the Platonic philosophy, however, the world of the millenium is not something to be brought about in the real world. Rather, it is a permanently co-existing contrast to that world, or at least to all of it that is evil. And here, perhaps, one can see how misleading it is, to say that

Shelley's last works are progressively less and less about the real world. What in essence they do, what everyone, Platonist or not, can accept them as doing, is to employ the ideas of Plato as sustained *metaphors*, through which to reveal, with decisive emphasis, the actualities and the potentialities of life, and the gulf between these. In *Adonais* the contrast is between a world in which a writer like Keats is ignored or reviled, and one in which the whole creation, in all its beauty and dignity, would mourn for his death and would unite with what he stood for. In *The Witch of Atlas*, and more solemnly in *The Triumph of Life*, the contrast is a world of drudging routine, power politics, superstition, and the enslavement of men by their passions, against one in which a spirit of love transfigures everything to serene beauty and ordered strength. To express these ideals may be a dream; but not an idle dream.

VI

Few single works of literature depict either the actualities or the potentialities of life in full. Those of Shelley certainly do not. It is along these lines, though, that one can most easily see their wide and real significance. Their import is by no means to be mere re-statements of the doctrines of Plato; it is to show, with compelling intensity, what men have made of life against what they might make of it. Certainly, Shelley himself would have wanted his poems to be taken as impinging seriously and significantly on the real affairs of men; and certainly it is along these lines that he would readily have seen them as doing so. This is clear from a passage in his Preface to *Prometheus Unbound*:

> It is a mistake to suppose that I dedicated my poetical compositions solely to the direct enforcement of reform, or that I consider them in any degree as containing a reasoned system on the theory of human life. Didactic poetry is my abhorrence; nothing can be equally well

expressed in prose that is not tedious and supererogatory in verse. My purpose has hitherto been simply to familiarize . . . the more select classes of poetical readers with *beautiful idealisms of moral excellence*; aware that until the mind can love, and admire, and trust, and hope and endure, reasoned principles of moral conduct are seeds cast upon the highway of life which the unconscious passenger tramples into dust, although they would bear the harvest of his happiness.

Clearly the word 'idealism' means something like 'imaginary picture'. It cannot be a realistic picture, because it is of something which excels reality. The same opinion is central in Shelley's *Defence of Poetry*. Here, beginning with an account of the nature of poetry, Shelley proceeds to an estimate of 'its effects upon society'. It is literature as a great moral power which concerns him; and his essential point is that literature is a great moral power not through straightforward instructing, not through making moral discriminations and passing judgements favourable or unfavourable upon the ordinary actions of men, but through operating at an altogether profounder level, and enlarging the very powers of mind by which these discriminations and judgements are to be made:

Ethical science arranges the elements . . . propounds schemes and proposes examples of civil and domestic life: nor is it for want of admirable doctrines that men hate, and despise, and censure, and deceive, and subjugate one another. But poetry acts in another and diviner manner. It awakens and enlarges the mind itself by rendering it the receptacle of a thousand unapprehended combinations of thought. Poetry lifts the veil from the hidden beauty of the world. . . . A man, to be greatly good, must imagine intensely and comprehensively; he must put himself in the place of another and of many others; the pains and pleasures of his species must become his own. The great instrument of moral good is the imagination; and poetry administers to the effect by acting upon the cause. Poetry enlarges the circumference of the imagination by replenishing it with thoughts of ever new delight . . .

This conception of the moral impact of poetry is more optimistic and ambitious than, say, Matthew Arnold's assertion that poetry should be 'interpretative and fortifying'. The latter was thinking of how poetry could help to introduce order and composure into a situation of moral uncertainty and debility; the former of how it could lead men forward from the moral awareness they had, to one always higher and more imaginative.

Indeed, it is exactly this which Shelley is advancing in the *Defence* as his chief general claim for poetry and poets throughout history; as against Peacock (to whom he was specifically retorting), who had argued in *The Four Ages of Poetry* that with the development of science and the other discursive disciplines of thought, poetry had become a futile survival from an age when men's intellectual equipment had been amateurish and primitive. Shelley's argument, supported by examples like that of Dante in the matter of idealized love between men and women, and Milton in that of the freedom of the mind, is that the opposite of what Peacock says is the truth. Poets (he is using the word in at least as wide a sense as we often use the word 'artist' to-day) have always led the rest of mankind in moral opinion: and they have led them in this because they led them in imaginative insight. What they see first, with the poet's eye, is later systematized by thinkers, codified by lawyers, practised (or evaded, of course) by men at large. This is the train of thought, far from true without qualification but certainly precise and deserving of reflection, which he sums up in his oft-ridiculed closing words, 'poets are the unacknowledged legislators of the world'. In this connexion, one unexpected fact is clear. It is customary to dismiss Shelley's own political thought as immature and enthusiastic; but the claim to be an unacknowledged legislator is one which can be substantiated fully for himself. The 'wild' writing which his sage detractors shake their heads over culminates in practical proposals (the abolition of the National Debt through, in effect, progressive taxation, civil non-violence, universal suffrage, equality for women, racial and religious toleration, intellectual freedom, a minimum standard of living) which are now simply the main social values that, between Shelley's time and our own, have been written into our national life until we take them for granted.

<h1 style="text-align:center">VII</h1>

In the situation which exists to-day, when Shelley is likely to be relied on by every budding critic as a safe quarry from which to chip specimens of almost any kind of poetic ineptitude, this discussion has concentrated on disposing of some of the hostile errors about Shelley, and on bringing out the coherence and reality of his work. Since a true perspective, however, is by no means of necessity created through erasing the caricatures of others, something remains to be said or at least to be underlined. In the first place, although his achievement as a poet is altogether outstanding, although there is a sense in which his work is more clearly irreplaceable than the work of greater poets, I think it must be recognized that in another sense his achievement is a clearly limited or perhaps one should say de-limited one. This is not to point out that much of his early work is prosy declamation. That is obvious enough. But even in his later work, the kinds of thing that he can do, the notes that he can strike, the aspects or areas of human life which he can exploit or illuminate at least directly, do not spread very wide. The recurrent quality of his images, his situations, has often been noticed. Again, *The Mask of Anarchy* is more like *Prometheus Unbound* than perhaps it should be, in view of its utterly different intention and *genre*. Johnson's phrase 'the want of human interest is always felt' is one which comes to mind. As it stands, it does not fit the case; as I have argued already. Yet a want of human interest created directly, created simply, coming not from a great effort but, let us say, from those corners of the poem which the writer seems to have completed with least effort of all—this kind of human interest, and the relaxing reassurance that it brings, is indeed to some extent wanting. It is certainly not always wanting, as some of the poems which follow put beyond dispute. But by comparison with many other poets of equal genius, it is not really conspicuous in Shelley. That his dramatic work (*Prometheus Unbound* is in a quite special class) is not among his best has its relevance here. There are some poets whose minds, and whose work, have spread so wide, that as we read them and become immersed in them, they begin to create an impression that what they have produced is something approaching not merely a *speculum vitae*, but a *speculum artis* as well. It is an exaggeration, yet the sensation grows in us that if all other poetry were lost, men could at least make this corpus of work, by this one man, lead outwards to most or all that poetry can do. Chaucer, Milton and Yeats (there is no need to invoke Shakespeare) seem all to be more or less of this kind: beauty, learning, good and evil in life, humour, satire, indignation, an understanding and sometimes a love of individual people and their meanest doings, a grasp of the affairs of states and of men, and many other things beside, seem all to enter their work with mastered ease. Shelley is not among them. His work is as remarkable as theirs, but decisively less capacious. He is not, to use his own words once again, among

> . . . the great bards of elder time, who quelled
> The passions that they sung, as by their strain
> May well be known.
>
> (*The Triumph of Life*, 274–6)

There is something else too, which that quotation points to clearly: in one respect, the limitation of range on what Shelley could achieve peculiarly increases the difficulty and reduces the pleasure of reading him. Shelley himself has diagnosed the matter far better than those who rely upon the word 'immature', which is no diagnosis at all, but merely a form of self-insurance. 'I cannot but be conscious, in much of what I write, of an absence of *that tranquillity which is the attribute and accompaniment of power*' (letter to Godwin; my italics). This is a very penetrating remark, both in particular and in general. The fact is, Shelley is hard to read not only because his language and indeed his punctuation are not quite our own, not only because what he intends to convey is sometimes condensed and esoteric, not only because his intelligence is dexterous enough, and in evidence enough, often to make what he writes more intricate than the work of others. It is difficult because there is, with trying regularity, a tension and an eagerness about it that leads the reader hardly to expect the control which he very often finds. One might almost put this point by saying that Shelley's sensibility was too emphatically unified to be altogether tolerable. No one ought to feel so passionately, so intensely as this, and yet move in thought with such virtuosity. Or perhaps it is better put as an excessive demand which Shelley makes on his readers; but it is not an excess merely in the sense of being above the powers of ordinary able men, it is an excess in which there is a hint of eccentricity, or rather of hypertrophy. If these powers are to be as great as these, others must suffer—a price is to be paid. Often enough in Shelley, and on a final judgement, I think, over his work seen as a whole, the price is a fatiguing intensity of intellectual and emotional response, within a range which is fatiguing in its narrowness. Only in *The Triumph of Life*, at the very end of his career, does one hear, sustained throughout a long and wholly serious work, that note of composure and calm, and indeed of dry shrewdness, which offers the reader of this very difficult poem a kind of reassurance new in Shelley. For this reason, he will never be universally admired; and his readers will be those prepared to experience a certain strain or discomfort for the things where he was a master.

That Shelley's achievement should not spread wide is no surprise. He died at an age when Yeats's work was crowned by *The Countess Kathleen*, Hopkins's by *The Habit of Perfection*, Milton's by *Lycidas*, Shakespeare's by (shall we say) *Romeo and Juliet*, Spenser's by *The Shepheardes Calender*, and Chaucer's by *The Boke of the Duchesse*. Were these the challenges he had to meet, Shelley's standing would be high indeed. As it is, I think there has by now been enough hasty and hubristic denigration of him, and of growing blind to the wood through zeal for felling the trees. The time has come when we should see him truthfully: a man who championed many good things which we now take for granted, at a time when everything seemed against them; and a poet who, clearly great though (as is equally clear) not supremely great, produced a body of work which occupies a major and highly distinctive place in our literature.

SUMMARY

SHELLEY'S LIFE AND LITERARY DEVELOPMENT

NOTE: Illustrative quotations, unless otherwise stated, are from Shelley's *Letters*. For portraits of Shelley's daily life at various times, see the *Letter to Maria Gisborne* (p. 5) and *The Boat on the Serchio* (p. 1).

4th August 1792, born at Field Place, Horsham, Sussex, the seat of his father Sir Timothy Shelley, Bart.

Educated at Sion Academy (1802–4) and Eton (1804–10) where he becomes absorbed in science. Another enthusiasm is the 'Gothick' novel: writes *Zastrozzi*, 1809, and reads Godwin's romances.

April 1810, goes to University College, Oxford. Begins friendship with T. J. Hogg (who gives an account of Shelley's college rooms full of scientific apparatus, etc.).
Enthusiastically reads Godwin's *Political Justice* ('a turning-point').

March 1811, expelled for refusing to deny authorship of a pamphlet, *The Necessity of Atheism*. Visits Wales. In August, in Edinburgh, weds Harriet Westbrook, daughter of a London coffee-house keeper-owner ('a Scottish marriage').

December 1811, meets Southey in Keswick, but disillusioned by his reactionary views.

January 1812, opens correspondence with Godwin. February–April, visits Ireland, and distributes his radical *Address to the Irish People* in Dublin.

June, July 1812, in a letter to Godwin, condemns classical studies as producing 'narrow bigots'.

Autumn 1812, through his publisher, Hookham, meets T. L. Peacock in London.

February 1813, Leigh Hunt and his brother imprisoned and fined for treason, viz., describing the Prince Regent, in an article in their paper *The Examiner*, as 'a fat Adonis of fifty' ('I am boiling with indignation').

Summer 1813, *Queen Mab*, with long philosophical and other notes, printed at Shelley's expense.

Autumn, with Peacock at Bracknell near Windsor, and in Edinburgh. Enthusiasm for classical studies begins under his influence. This winter Hogg records Shelley reading Homer by firelight 'until his cheek was red as an apple'.

18th June 1814, makes his first call at Godwin's house.

28th July 1814, Shelley and Mary Godwin, with Mary's half-sister, Claire Clairmont, 'elope', cross to the Continent, reach Lucerne. They return to England in September.

January 1815, Shelley's income much increased through the death of his grandfather. Large money gifts to Godwin begin. (Later, 1819, 'I have bought bitter knowledge with £4700').

Autumn-winter, 1815-16, Shelley at Windsor, Peacock at Marlow, walking together and talking Hellenism. *Alastor* is written: Shelley's first important non-political poem.

January 1816, Mary's first child, William, born.

April 1816, the Byron scandal: Byron leaves for the Continent. In May, Shelley and Mary join Byron at Geneva, where they spend the summer together. Mary writes her 'terror' novel *Frankenstein*.

Autumn 1816, they return, settle at Marlow, Shelley meets Leigh Hunt and his acquaintance with the 'Cockney School' and Keats begins.

November 1816, suicide of Harriet Shelley in the Serpentine. Shelley and Mary now marry.

27th March 1817, Lord Chancellor Eldon allots the custody of Harriet's children (Ianthe, born June 1813; Charles Bysshe, born November 1814) to Harriet's sister and father. (Shelley is considered unfit as an atheist and believer in free love. Mary's child William seems threatened by this decision, and also the second child, Clara, born September 1817.)

Autumn 1817, friendship with Leigh Hunt grows ('I have firm friends here').

4th February 1818, Shelley, Keats, and Leigh Hunt, at Hunt's cottage near Hampstead, write sonnets to the Nile in competition. *The Revolt of Islam* was probably written April–September 1817 in friendly competition with Keats's *Endymion*.

11th March 1818, the Shelleys leave England for Italy. During the summer, in Lucca, Shelley translates Plato's *Symposium* ('I have been reading scarcely anything but Greek, and a little Italian poetry with Mary': 25th July).

Autumn 1818, goes to Venice to take Byron his daughter Allegra. During this trip, Shelley's daughter Clara dies. *Lines Written Among the Euganean Hills* (Este, October), composed with this in mind.

Winter 1818–19, visits Rome, Naples, Pompeii, and the Greek temples at Paestum.

Spring 1819, in Rome, writes *Prometheus Unbound* ('a poem in my best style, whatever that may amount to ... the most perfect of my productions': S. writes this in October 1819). Also *The Cenci* ('I have written a tragedy . . . what I want you to do is, to procure for me its presentation at Covent Garden'; to Peacock, July).

June 1819, the Shelleys move to Florence, where their son William dies. News of the Peterloo Massacre (August) causes Shelley to write *The Mask of Anarchy* (p. 18). *Ode to the West Wind* written (October) after watching a thunderstorm from the woods near Florence. (The feelings expressed in this poem are not unconnected with a striking passage in a letter of August: 'I most devoutly wish we were living near London. . . . My inclinations point to Hampstead; but I do not know whether I should not make up my mind to something more completely suburban [i.e., Hampstead was then an outer suburb]. What are mountains, trees, heaths, or even the glorious and ever-beautiful sky, with such sunsets as I have seen at Hampstead, to friends? Social enjoyment, in some form or other, is the alpha and the omega of existence.')

November 1819, Shelley's long letter to Hunt (for publication) on the trial for treason of the radical printer Carlile. Birth of the Shelleys' third child, Percy Florence (who succeeded to Shelley's father's baronetcy).

End 1819, move to Pisa, growing friendship with the Gisbornes and with Mrs. Gisborne's son by her first marriage, Henry Reveley, an engineer planning a steamboat service between Leghorn and Genoa.
Shelley meets Sophia Stacey (*The Indian Serenade, To —*, pp. 38, 40).

July 1820, while staying in the Gisbornes' house during their visit to London, S. writes the *Letter to Maria Gisborne* (p. 5), *The Cloud* (p. 52), and *To a Skylark* (p. 43). ('I am told that the magazines, etc., blaspheme me at a great rate. I wonder why I write verses, for nobody reads them'.)
S. writes to Keats, inviting him to join them in Italy. Keats amiably declines. ('I am aware, indeed, in part, that I am nourishing a rival who will far surpass me; and this is an additional motive, and will be an added pleasure', November 1820.)

December 1820, Shelley meets Emilia Viviani, about whom he writes *Epipsychidion*, 1821.

January 1821, death of Keats in Rome. On hearing the news some weeks later, Shelley begins his elegy, *Adonais* (p. 57) ('In spite of its mysticism, the least imperfect of my compositions, and . . . the image of my regret and honour for poor Keats'.)

S. writes *The Defence of Poetry* as a detailed answer to Peacock's satirical *Four Ages of Poetry*, published in the opening number of *Ollier's Magazine* (Ollier was Shelley's publisher). The Shelleys make friends with Edward and Jane Williams (*To Jane*, p. 40).

April 1821, outbreak of the Greek War for Independence. Shelley writes his drama *Hellas* at Pisa in the autumn.

October, *Peter Bell the Third* written. ('I think *Peter* not bad in his way; but perhaps no one will believe in anything in the shape of a joke from me'.)

November, the Williamses move into Shelley's house at Pisa. Edward acts as amanuensis for Shelley who is translating Spinoza's *Tractatus Theologico-Politicus*.

1st March 1822, the Shelleys and the Williamses move to the Casa Magni, San Terenzo, Lerici, in the gulf of Spezzia. S. works on *The Triumph of Life* (p. 100).

2nd July 1822, at Leghorn, Shelley meets Hunt, who had come out to Italy (with his large family) to help S. and Byron edit a radical journal.

8th July, S. and Williams, sailing back to Lerici, are drowned at sea when Shelley's boat (the 'Don Juan') founders in a storm. The bodies are discovered washed ashore some days later. Permission was given to bury Shelley's remains at Rome provided that he was cremated; this, attended by Byron, Hunt and others, was done on the sands at the mouth of the river Serchio (where Shelley was at first buried) on 16th August 1822.

The Boat on the Serchio

Our boat is asleep on Serchio's stream,
Its sails are folded like thoughts in a dream,
The helm sways idly, hither and thither;
   Dominic, the boatman, has brought the mast,
    And the oars, and the sails; but 'tis sleeping fast,
Like a beast, unconscious of its tether.

The stars burnt out in the pale blue air,
And the thin white moon lay withering there;
To tower, and cavern, and rift, and tree,
The owl and the bat fled drowsily.   10
Day had kindled the dewy woods,
   And the rocks above and the stream below,
And the vapours in their multitudes,
   And the Apennines' shroud of summer snow,
And clothed with light of aëry gold
The mists in their eastern caves uprolled.

Day had awakened all things that be,
The lark and the thrush and the swallow free,
   And the milkmaid's song and the mower's scythe,
And the matin-bell and the mountain bee: 20
Fireflies were quenched on the dewy corn,
   Glow-worms went out on the river's brim,
   Like lamps which a student forgets to trim:
The beetle forgot to wind his horn,
   The crickets were still in the meadow and hill:

Like a flock of rooks at a farmer's gun
Night's dreams and terrors, every one,
Fled from the brains which are their prey
From the lamp's death to the morning ray.

All rose to do the task He set to each,   30
   Who shaped us to his ends and not our own;
The million rose to learn, and one to teach
   What none yet ever knew or can be known.
     And many rose
   Whose woe was such that fear became desire;—
Melchior and Lionel were not among those;
They from the throng of men had stepped aside,
And made their home under the green hill-side.
It was that hill, whose intervening brow
   Screens Lucca from the Pisan's envious eye,   40
Which the circumfluous plain waving below,
   Like a wide lake of green fertility,
With streams and fields and marshes bare,
   Divides from the far Apennines—which lie
Islanded in the immeasurable air.

'What think you, as she lies in her green cove,
Our little sleeping boat is dreaming of?'
'If morning dreams are true, why I should guess
That she was dreaming of our idleness,
And of the miles of watery way   50
We should have led her by this time of day.'—

   'Never mind,' said Lionel,
   'Give care to the winds, they can bear it well
About yon poplar-tops; and see
The white clouds are driving merrily,
And the stars we miss this morn will light
More willingly our return to-night.—

How it whistles, Dominic's long black hair!
List, my dear fellow; the breeze blows fair:
Hear how it sings into the air—'   60

—'Of us and of our lazy motions,'
    Impatiently said Melchior,
'If I can guess a boat's emotions;
    And how we ought, two hours before,
To have been the devil knows where.'
And then, in such transalpine Tuscan
As would have killed a Della-Cruscan,

So, Lionel according to his art
    Weaving his idle words, Melchior said:
    'She dreams that we are not yet out of bed;   70
We'll put a soul into her, and a heart
Which like a dove chased by a dove shall beat.'

        'Ay, heave the ballast overboard,
    And stow the eatables in the aft locker.'
'Would not this keg be best a little lowered?'
'No, now all's right.' 'Those bottles of warm tea—
(Give me some straw)—must be stowed tenderly;
Such as we used in summer after six,
To cram in greatcoat pockets, and to mix
Hard eggs and radishes and rolls at Eton,   80
And, couched on stolen hay in those green harbours
Farmers called gaps, and we schoolboys called arbours,
Would feast till eight.'

        With a bottle in one hand,
As if his very soul were at a stand,
Lionel stood—when Melchior brought him steady:—
'Sit at the helm—fasten this sheet—all ready!'

The chain is loosed, the sails are spread,
  The living breath is fresh behind,
As, with dews and sunrise fed,   90
  Comes the laughing morning wind;—
The sails are full, the boat makes head
Against the Serchio's torrent fierce,
Then flags with intermitting course,
  And hangs upon the wave, and stems
  The tempest of the . . .
Which fervid from its mountain source
Shallow, smooth and strong doth come,—
Swift as fire, tempestuously
It sweeps into the affrighted sea;   100
In morning's smile its eddies coil,
Its billows sparkle, toss and boil,
Torturing all its quiet light
Into columns fierce and bright.

      The Serchio, twisting forth
Between the marble barriers which it clove
  At Ripafratta, leads through the dread chasm
The wave that died the death which lovers love,
  Living in what it sought; as if this spasm
Had not yet passed, the toppling mountains cling,   110
  But the clear stream in full enthusiasm
Pours itself on the plain, then wandering
  Down one clear path of effluence crystalline
Sends its superfluous waves, that they may fling
  At Arno's feet tribute of corn and wine;
Then, through the pestilential deserts wild
  Of tangled marsh and woods of stunted pine,
It rushes to the Ocean.

Letter to Maria Gisborne

(LEGHORN, JULY 1, 1820)

The spider spreads her webs, whether she be
In poet's tower, cellar, or barn, or tree;
The silk-worm in the dark green mulberry leaves
His winding sheet and cradle ever weaves;
So I, a thing whom moralists call worm,
Sit spinning still round this decaying form,
From the fine threads of rare and subtle thought--
No net of words in garish colours wrought
To catch the idle buzzers of the day—
But a soft cell, where when that fades away,   10
Memory may clothe in wings my living name
And feed it with the asphodels of fame,
Which in those hearts which must remember me
Grow, making love an immortality.

Whoever should behold me now, I wist,
Would think I were a mighty mechanist,
Bent with sublime Archimedean art
To breathe a soul into the iron heart
Of some machine portentous, or strange gin,
Which by the force of figured spells might win   20
Its way over the sea, and sport therein;
For round the walls are hung dread engines, such
As Vulcan never wrought for Jove to clutch
Ixion or the Titan:—or the quick
Wit of that man of God, St. Dominic,

To convince Atheist, Turk, or Heretic,
Or those in philanthropic council met,
Who thought to pay some interest for the debt
They owed to Jesus Christ for their salvation,
By giving a faint foretaste of damnation 30
To Shakespeare, Sidney, Spenser, and the rest
Who made our land an island of the blest,
When lamp-like Spain, who now relumes her fire
On Freedom's hearth, grew dim with Empire:—
With thumbscrews, wheels, with tooth and spike and jag,
Which fishers found under the utmost crag
Of Cornwall and the storm-encompassed isles,
Where to the sky the rude sea rarely smiles
Unless in treacherous wrath, as on the morn
When the exulting elements in scorn, 40
Satiated with destroyed destruction, lay
Sleeping in beauty on their mangled prey,
As panthers sleep;—and other strange and dread
Magical forms the brick floor overspread,—
Proteus transformed to metal did not make
More figures, or more strange; nor did he take
Such shapes of unintelligible brass,
Or heap himself in such a horrid mass
Of tin and iron not to be understood;
And forms of unimaginable wood, 50
To puzzle Tubal Cain and all his brood:
Great screws, and cones, and wheels, and grovèd blocks,
The elements of what will stand the shocks
Of wave and wind and time.—Upon the table
More knacks and quips there be than I am able
To catalogize in this verse of mine:—
A pretty bowl of wood—not full of wine,
But quicksilver; that dew which the gnomes drink
When at their subterranean toil they swink,

Pledging the demons of the earthquake, who
Reply to them in lava—cry halloo!
And call out to the cities o'er their head,—
Roofs, towers, and shrines, the dying and the dead,
Crash through the chinks of earth—and then all quaff
Another rouse, and hold their sides and laugh.
This quicksilver no gnome has drunk—within
The walnut bowl it lies, veinèd and thin,
In colour like the wake of light that stains
The Tuscan deep, when from the moist moon rains
The inmost shower of its white fire—the breeze
Is still—blue Heaven smiles over the pale seas.
And in this bowl of quicksilver—for I
Yield to the impulse of an infancy
Outlasting manhood—I have made to float
A rude idealism of a paper boat:—
A hollow screw with cogs—Henry will know
The thing I mean and laugh at me,—if so
He fears not I should do more mischief.—Next
Lie bills and calculations much perplexed,
With steam-boats, frigates, and machinery quaint
Traced over them in blue and yellow paint.
Then comes a range of mathematical
Instruments, for plans nautical and statical;
A heap of rosin, a queer broken glass
With ink in it;—a china cup that was
What it will never be again, I think,—
A thing from which sweet lips were wont to drink
The liquor doctors rail at—and which I
Will quaff in spite of them—and when we die
We'll toss up who died first of drinking tea,
And cry out,—'Heads or tails?' where'er we be.
Near that a dusty paint-box, some odd hooks,
A half-burnt match, an ivory block, three books,

Where conic sections, spherics, logarithms,
To great Laplace, from Saunderson and Sims,
Lie heaped in their harmonious disarray
Of figures,—disentangle them who may.
Baron de Tott's Memoirs beside them lie,
And some odd volumes of old chemistry.
Near those a most inexplicable thing,   100
With lead in the middle—I'm conjecturing
How to make Henry understand; but no—
I'll leave, as Spenser says, with many mo,
This secret in the pregnant womb of time,
Too vast a matter for so weak a rhyme.

    And here like some weird Archimage sit I,
Plotting dark spells, and devilish enginery,
The self-impelling steam-wheels of the mind
Which pump up oaths from clergymen, and grind
The gentle spirit of our meek reviews   110
Into a powdery foam of salt abuse,
Ruffling the ocean of their self-content;—
I sit—and smile or sigh as is my bent,
But not for them—Libeccio rushes round
With an inconstant and an idle sound,
I heed him more than them—the thunder-smoke
Is gathering on the mountains, like a cloak
Folded athwart their shoulders broad and bare;
The ripe corn under the undulating air
Undulates like an ocean;—and the vines   120
Are trembling wide in all their trellised lines—
The murmur of the awakening sea doth fill
The empty pauses of the blast;—the hill
Looks hoary through the white electric rain,
And from the glens beyond, in sullen strain,
The interrupted thunder howls; above

One chasm of Heaven smiles, like the eye of Love
On the unquiet world;—while such things are,
How could one worth your friendship heed the
    war
Of worms? the shriek of the world's carrion jays,   130
Their censure, or their wonder, or their praise?

You are not here! the quaint witch Memory sees,
In vacant chairs, your absent images,
And points where once you sat, and now should be
But are not.—I demand if ever we
Shall meet as then we met;—and she replies,
Veiling in awe her second-sighted eyes;
'I know the past alone—but summon home
My sister Hope,—she speaks of all to come.'
But I, an old diviner, who knew well   140
Every false verse of that sweet oracle,
Turned to the sad enchantress once again,
And sought a respite from my gentle pain,
In citing every passage o'er and o'er
Of our communion—how on the sea-shore
We watched the ocean and the sky together,
Under the roof of blue Italian weather;
How I ran home through last year's thunder-storm,
And felt the transverse lightning linger warm
Upon my cheek—and how we often made   150
Feasts for each other, where good will outweighed
The frugal luxury of our country cheer,
As well it might, were it less firm and clear
Than ours must ever be;—and how we spun
A shroud of talk to hide us from the sun
Of this familiar life, which seems to be
But is not:—or is but quaint mockery
Of all we would believe, and sadly blame

9

The jarring and inexplicable frame
Of this wrong world:—and then anatomize
The purposes and thoughts of men whose eyes
Were closed in distant years;—or widely guess
The issue of the earth's great business,
When we shall be as we no longer are—
Like babbling gossips safe, who hear the war
Of winds, and sigh, but tremble not;—or how
You listened to some interrupted flow
Of visionary rhyme,—in joy and pain
Struck from the inmost fountains of my brain,
With little skill perhaps;—or how we sought 170
Those deepest wells of passion or of thought
Wrought by wise poets in the waste of years,
Staining their sacred waters with our tears;
Quenching a thirst ever to be renewed!
Or how I, wisest lady! then endued
The language of a land which now is free,
And, winged with thoughts of truth and majesty,
Flits round the tyrant's sceptre like a cloud,
And bursts the peopled prisons, and cries aloud,
'My name is Legion!'—that majestic tongue 180
Which Calderon over the desert flung
Of ages and of nations; and which found
An echo in our hearts, and with the sound
Startled oblivion;—thou wert then to me
As is a nurse—when inarticulately
A child would talk as its grown parents do.
If living winds the rapid clouds pursue,
If hawks chase doves through the aethereal way,
Huntsmen the innocent deer, and beasts their prey,
Why should not we rouse with the spirit's blast 190
Out of the forest of the pathless past
These recollected pleasures?

10

                    You are now
In London, that great sea, whose ebb and flow
At once is deaf and loud, and on the shore
Vomits its wrecks, and still howls on for more.
Yet in its depth what treasures! You will see
That which was Godwin,—greater none than he
Though fallen—and fallen on evil times—to stand
Among the spirits of our age and land,
Before the dread tribunal of *to come*   200
The foremost,—while Rebuke cowers pale and dumb.
You will see Coleridge—he who sits obscure
In the exceeding lustre and the pure
Intense irradiation of a mind,
Which, with its own internal lightning blind,
Flags wearily through darkness and despair—
A cloud-encircled meteor of the air,
A hooded eagle among blinking owls.—
You will see Hunt—one of thoes happy souls
Which are the salt of the earth, and without whom   210
This world would smell like what it is—a tomb;
Who is, what others seem; his room no doubt
Is still adorned with many a cast from Shout,
With graceful flowers tastefully placed about;
And coronals of bay from ribbons hung,
And brighter wreaths in neat disorder flung;
The gifts of the most learned among some dozens
Of female friends, sisters-in-law, and cousins.
And there is he with his eternal puns,
Which beat the dullest brain for smiles, like duns   220
Thundering for money at a poet's door;
Alas! it is no use to say, 'I'm poor!'
Or oft in graver mood, when he will look
Things wiser than were ever read in book,
Except in Shakespeare's wisest tenderness.—

You will see Hogg,—and I cannot express
His virtues,—though I know that they are great,
Because he locks, then barricades the gate
Within which they inhabit;—of his wit
And wisdom, you'll cry out when you are bit.   230
He is a pearl within an oyster shell,
One of the richest of the deep;—and there
Is English Peacock, with his mountain Fair,
Turned into a Flamingo;—that shy bird
That gleams i' the Indian air—have you not heard
When a man marries, dies, or turns Hindoo,
His best friends hear no more of him?—but you
Will see him, and will like him too, I hope,
With the milk-white Snowdonian Antelope
Matched with this cameleopard—his fine wit   240
Makes such a wound, the knife is lost in it;
A strain too learnèd for a shallow age,
Too wise for selfish bigots; let his page,
Which charms the chosen spirits of the time,
Fold itself up for the serener clime
Of years to come, and find its recompense
In that just expectation.—Wit and sense,
Virtue and human knowledge; all that might
Make this dull world a business of delight,
Are all combined in Horace Smith.—And these,   250
With some exceptions, which I need not tease
Your patience by descanting on,—are all
You and I know in London.
                              I recall
My thoughts, and bid you look upon the night.
As water does a sponge, so the moonlight
Fills the void, hollow, universal air—
What see you?—unpavilioned Heaven is fair,

Whether the moon, into her chamber gone,
Leaves midnight to the golden stars, or wan
Climbs with diminished beams the azure steep;   260
Or whether clouds sail o'er the inverse deep,
Piloted by the many wandering blast,
And the rare stars rush through them dim and fast:—
All this is beautiful in every land.—
But what see you beside?—a shabby stand
Of Hackney coaches—a brick house or wall
Fencing some lonely court, white with the scrawl
Of our unhappy politics;—or worse—
A wretched woman reeling by, whose curse
Mixed with the watchman's, partner of her trade,   270
You must accept in place of serenade—
Or yellow-haired Pollonia murmuring
To Henry, some unutterable thing.
I see a chaos of green leaves and fruit
Built round dark caverns, even to the root
Of the living stems that feed them—in whose bowers
There sleep in their dark dew the folded flowers;
Beyond, the surface of the unsickled corn
Trembles not in the slumbering air, and borne
In circles quaint, and ever-changing dance,   280
Like wingèd stars the fire-flies flash and glance,
Pale in the open moonshine, but each one
Under the dark trees seems a little sun,
A meteor tamed; a fixed star gone astray
From the silver regions of the milky way;—
Afar the Contadino's song is heard,
Rude, but made sweet by distance—and a bird
Which cannot be the Nightingale, and yet
I know none else that sings so sweet as it
At this late hour;—and then all is still—   290
Now—Italy or London, which you will!

13

Next winter you must pass with me; I'll have
My house by that time turned into a grave
Of dead despondence and low-thoughted care,
And all the dreams which our tormentors are;
Oh! that Hunt, Hogg, Peacock, and Smith were there,
With everything belonging to them fair!—
We will have books, Spanish, Italian, Greek;
And ask one week to make another week
As like his father, as I'm unlike mine,   300
Which is not his fault, which you may divine.
Though we eat little flesh and drink no wine,
Yet let's be merry: we'll have tea and toast;
Costards for supper, and an endless host
Of syllabubs and jellies and mince-pies,
And other such lady-like luxuries,—
Feasting on which we will philosophize!
And we'll have fires out of the Grand Duke's wood,
To thaw the six weeks' winter in our blood.
And then we'll talk;—what shall we talk about?   310
Oh! there are themes enough for many a bout
Of thought-entangled descant;—as to nerves—
With cones and parallelograms and curves
I've sworn to strangle them if once they dare
To bother me—when you are with me there.
And they shall never more sip laudanum,
From Helicon or Himeros[1] ;—well, come,
And in despite of God and of the devil,
We'll make our friendly philosophic revel
Outlast the leafless time; till buds and flowers   320
Warn the obscure inevitable hours,
Sweet meeting by sad parting to renew;—
'To-morrow to fresh woods and pastures new.'

[1] Ἵμερος, from which the river Himera was named, is, with some slight shade
of difference, a synonym of Love.—(Shelley's Note).

The Aziola

'Do you not hear the Aziola cry?
   Methinks she must be nigh,'
    Said Mary, as we sate
In dusk, ere stars were lit, or candles brought;
    And I, who thought
  This Aziola was some tedious woman,
   Asked, 'Who is Aziola?' How elate
  I felt to know that it was nothing human,
   No mockery of myself to fear or hate:
    And Mary saw my soul,   10
And laughed, and said, 'Disquiet yourself not;
   'Tis nothing but a little downy owl.'

Sad Aziola! many an eventide
   Thy music I had heard
By wood and stream, meadow and mountain-side,
   And fields and marshes wide,—
Such as nor voice, nor lute, nor wind, nor bird,
   The soul ever stirred;
Unlike and far sweeter than them all.
Sad Aziola! from that moment I   20
   Loved thee and thy sad cry.

Sonnet: England in 1819

An old, mad, blind, despised, and dying king,—
Princes, the dregs of their dull race, who flow
Through public scorn,—mud from a muddy spring,—
Rulers who neither see, nor feel, nor know,
But leech-like to their fainting country cling,
Till they drop, blind in blood, without a blow,—
A people starved and stabbed in the untilled field,—
An army, which liberticide and prey
Makes as a two-edged sword to all who wield,—
Golden and sanguine laws which tempt and slay;
Religion Christless, Godless—a book sealed;
A Senate,—Time's worst statute unrepealed,—
Are graves, from which a glorious Phantom may
Burst, to illumine our tempestuous day.

From

The Devil's Walk

A Ballad

(PUBLISHED AS A BROADSIDE BY SHELLEY, 1812)

Once, early in the morning,
  Beelzebub arose,
With care his sweet person adorning,
  He put on his Sunday clothes.

He drew on a boot to hide his hoof,
   He drew on a glove to hide his claw,
His horns were concealed by a *Bras Chapeau*,
And the Devil went forth as natty a *Beau*
   As Bond-street ever saw.

He sate him down, in London town,
      Before earth's morning ray;
With a favourite imp he began to chat,
On religion, and scandal, this and that,
      Until the dawn of day.

And then to St. James's Court he went,
   And St. Paul's Church he took on his way;
He was mighty thick with every Saint,
   Though they were formal and he was gay. . . .

He peeped in each hole, to each chamber stole,
      His promising live-stock to view;
Grinning applause, he just showed them his claws,
And they shrunk with affright from his ugly sight,
      Whose work they delighted to do.

Satan poked his red nose into crannies so small
      One would think that the innocents fair,
Poor lambkins! were just doing nothing at all
But settling some dress or arranging some ball,
      But the Devil saw deeper there. . . .

The Mask of Anarchy

As I lay asleep in Italy
There came a voice from over the Sea,
And with great power it forth led me
To walk in the visions of Poesy.

I met Murder on the way—
He had a mask like Castlereagh—
Very smooth he looked, yet grim;
Seven blood-hounds followed him:

All were fat; and well they might
Be in admirable plight,   10
For one by one, and two by two,
He tossed them human hearts to chew
Which from his wide cloak he drew.

Next came Fraud, and he had on,
Like Eldon, an ermined gown;
His big tears, for he wept well,
Turned to mill-stones as they fell.

And the little children, who
Round his feet played to and fro,
Thinking every tear a gem,   20
Had their brains knocked out by them.

Clothed with the Bible, as with light,
And the shadows of the night,
Like Sidmouth, next, Hypocrisy
On a crocodile rode by.

And many more Destructions played
In this ghastly masquerade,
All disguised, even to the eyes,
Like Bishops, lawyers, peers, or spies.

Last came Anarchy: he rode   30
On a white horse, splashed with blood;
He was pale even to the lips,
Like Death in the Apocalypse.

And he wore a kingly crown;
And in his grasp a sceptre shone;
On his brow this mark I saw—
'I AM GOD, AND KING, AND LAW!'

With a pace stately and fast,
Over English land he passed,
Trampling to a mire of blood   40
The adoring multitude.

And a mighty troop around,
With their trampling shook the ground,
Waving each a bloody sword,
For the service of their Lord.

And with glorious triumph, they
Rode through England proud and gay,
Drunk as with intoxication
Of the wine of desolation.

O'er fields and towns, from sea to sea,   50
Passed the Pageant swift and free,
Tearing up, and trampling down;
Till they came to London town.

And each dweller, panic-stricken,
Felt his heart with terror sicken
Hearing the tempestuous cry
Of the triumph of Anarchy.

For with pomp to meet him came,
Clothed in arms like blood and flame,
The hired murderers, who did sing 60
'Thou art God, and Law, and King.

'We have waited, weak and lone
For thy coming, Mighty One!
Our purses are empty, our swords are cold,
Give us glory, and blood, and gold.'

Lawyers and priests, a motley crowd,
To the earth their pale brows bowed;
Like a bad prayer not over loud,
Whispering—'Thou art Law and God.'—

Then all cried with one accord, 70
'Thou art King, and God, and Lord;
Anarchy, to thee we bow,
Be thy name made holy now!'

And Anarchy, the Skeleton,
Bowed and grinned to every one,
As well as if his education
Has cost ten millions to the nation.

For he knew the Palaces
Of our Kings were rightly his;
His the sceptre, crown, and globe, 80
And the gold-inwoven robe.

So he sent his slaves before
To seize upon the Bank and Tower,
And was proceeding with intent
To mete his pensioned Parliament.

When one fled past, a maniac maid,
And her name was Hope, she said:
But she looked more like Despair,
And she cried out in the air:

'My father time is weak and gray   90
With waiting for a better day;
See how idiot-like he stands,
Fumbling with his palsied hands!

'He has had child after child,
And the dust of death is piled
Over every one but me—
Misery, oh, Misery!'

Then she lay down in the street,
Right before the horses' feet,
Expecting, with a patient eye,   100
Murder, Fraud, and Anarchy.

When between her and her foes
A mist, a light, an image rose,
Small at first, and weak, and frail
Like the vapour of a vale:

Till as clouds grow on the blast,
Like tower-crowned giants striding fast,
And glare with lightnings as they fly,
And speak in thunder to the sky,

It grew—a Shape arrayed in mail
Brighter than the viper's scale,
And upborne on wings whose grain
Was as the light of sunny rain.

On its helm, seen far away,
A planet, like the morning's, lay;
And those plumes its light rained through
Like a shower of crimson dew.

With step as soft as wind it passed
O'er the heads of men—so fast
That they knew the presence there,
And looked,—but all was empty air.

As flowers beneath May's footstep waken,
As stars from Night's loose hair are shaken,
As waves arise when loud winds call,
Thoughts sprung where'er that step did fall.

And the prostrate multitude
Looked—and ankle-deep in blood,
Hope, that maiden most serene,
Was walking with a quiet mien:

And Anarchy, the ghastly birth,
Lay dead earth upon the earth;
The Horse of Death tameless as wind
Fled, and with his hoofs did grind
To dust the murderers thronged behind.

A rushing light of clouds and splendour,
A sense awakening and yet tender
Was heard and felt—and at its close
Those words of joy and fear arose

As if their own indignant Earth
Which gave the sons of England birth   140
Has felt their blood upon her brow,
And shuddering with a mother's throe

Had turnèd every drop of blood
By which her face had been bedewed
To an accent unwithstood,—
As if her heart had cried aloud:

'Men of England, heirs of Glory,
Heroes of unwritten story,
Nurslings of one mighty Mother,
Hopes of her, and one another;   150

'Rise like Lions after slumber
In unvanquishable number,
Shake your chains to earth like dew
Which in sleep had fallen on you—
Ye are many—they are few.

'What is Freedom?—ye can tell
That which slavery is too well—
For its very name has grown
To an echo of your own.

''Tis to work and have such pay   160
As just keeps life from day to day
In your limbs, as in a cell
For the tyrants' use to dwell,

'So that ye for them are made
Loom, and plough, and sword, and spade,
With or without your own will bent
To their defence and nourishment.

"Tis to see your children weak
With their mothers pine and peak,
When the winter winds are bleak,--   170
They are dying whilst I speak.

"Tis to hunger for such diet
As the rich man in his riot
Casts to the fat dogs that lie
Surfeiting beneath his eye;

"Tis to let the Ghost of Gold
Take from Toil a thousandfold
More than e'er its substance could
In the tyrannies of old.

'Paper coin—that forgery   180
Of the title-deeds, which ye
Hold to something of the worth
Of the inheritance of Earth.

"Tis to be a slave in soul
And to hold no strong control
Over your own wills, but be
All that others make of ye.

'And at length when ye complain
With a murmur weak and vain
'Tis to see the Tyrant's crew   190
Ride over your wives and you—
Blood is on the grass like dew.

'Then it is to feel revenge
Fiercely thirsting to exchange
Blood for blood—and wrong for wrong —
Do not thus when ye are strong.

'Birds find rest, in narrow nest
When weary of their wingèd quest;
Beasts find fare, in woody lair
When storm and snow are in the air.   200

'Horses, oxen, have a home,
When from daily toil they come;
Household dogs, when the wind roars,
Find a home within warm doors.

'Asses, swine, have litter spread
And with fitting food are fed;
All things have a home but one—
Thou, Oh, Englishman, hast none!

'This is Slavery—savage men,
Or wild beasts within a den   210
Would endure not as ye do—
But such ills they never knew.

'What art thou, Freedom? O! could slaves
Answer from their living graves
This demand—tyrants would flee
Like a dream's dim imagery:

'Thou art not, as impostors say,
A shadow soon to pass away,
A superstition, and a name
Echoing from the cave of Fame.   220

'For the labourer thou art bread,
And a comely table spread
From his daily labour come
In a neat and happy home.

25

'Thou art clothes, and fire, and food
For the trampled multitude—
No—in countries that are free
Such starvation cannot be
As in England now we see.

'To the rich thou art a check,   230
When his foot is on the neck
Of his victim, thou dost make
That he treads upon a snake.

'Thou art Justice—ne'er for gold
May thy righteous laws be sold
As laws are in England—thou
Shield'st alike the high and low.

'Thou art Wisdom—Freemen never
Dream that God will damn for ever
All who think those things untrue   240
Of which Priests make such ado.

'Thou art Peace—never by thee
Would blood and treasure wasted be
As tyrants wasted them, when all
Leagued to quench thy flame in Gaul.

'What if English toil and blood
Was poured forth, even as a flood?
It availed, Oh, Liberty,
To dim, but not extinguish thee.

'Thou art Love—the rich have kissed   250
Thy feet, and like him following Christ,
Give their substance to the free
And through the rough world follow thee,

'Or turn their wealth to arms, and make
War for thy belovèd sake
On wealth, and war, and fraud—whence they
Drew the power which is their prey.

'Science, Poetry, and Thought
Are thy lamps; they make the lot
Of the dwellers in a cot   260
So serene, they curse it not.

'Spirit, Patience, Gentleness,
All that can adorn and bless
Art thou—let deeds, not words, express
Thine exceeding loveliness.

'Let a great Assembly be
Of the fearless and the free
On some spot of English ground
Where the plains stretch wide around.

'Let the blue sky overhead,   270
The green earth on which ye tread,
All that must eternal be
Witness the solemnity.

'From the corners uttermost
Of the bounds of English coast;
From every hut, village, and town
Where those who live and suffer moan
For others' misery or their own,

'From the workhouse and the prison
Where pale as corpses newly risen,   280
Women, children, young and old
Groan for pain, and weep for cold—

'From the haunts of daily life
Where is waged the daily strife
With common wants and common cares
Which sows the human heart with tares—

'Lastly from the palaces
Where the murmur of distress
Echoes, like the distant sound
Of a wind alive around   290

'Those prison halls of wealth and fashion,
Where some few feel such compassion
For those who groan, and toil, and wail
As must make their brethren pale—

'Ye who suffer woes untold,
Or to feel, or to behold
Your lost country bought and sold
With a price of blood and gold—

'Let a vast assembly be,
And with great solemnity   300
Declare with measured words that ye
Are, as God has made ye, free—

'Be your strong and simple words
Keen to wound as sharpened swords,
And wide as targes let them be,
With their shade to cover ye.

'Let the tyrants pour around
With a quick and startling sound,
Like the loosening of a sea,
Troops of armed emblazonry.   310

'Let the charged artillery drive
Till the dead air seems alive
With the clash of clanging wheels,
And the tramp of horses' heels.

'Let the fixèd bayonet
Gleam with sharp desire to wet
Its bright point in English blood
Looking keen as one for food.

'Let the horsemen's scimitars
Wheel and flash like sphereless stars   320
Thirsting to eclipse their burning
In a sea of death and mourning.

'Stand ye calm and resolute,
Like a forest close and mute,
With folded arms and looks which are
Weapons of unvanquished war,

'And let Panic, who outspeeds
The career of armèd steeds
Pass, a disregarded shade
Through your phalanx undismayed.   330

'Let the laws of your own land,
Good or ill, between ye stand
Hand to hand, and foot to foot,
Arbiters of the dispute,

'The old laws of England—they
Whose reverend heads with age are gray,
Children of a wiser day;
And whose solemn voice must be
Thine own echo—Liberty!

'On those who first should violate 340
Such sacred heralds in their state
Rest the blood that must ensue,
And it will not rest on you.

'And if then the tyrants dare
Let them ride among you there,
Slash, and stab, and maim, and hew,—
What they like, that let them do.

'With folded arms and steady eyes,
And little fear, and less surprise,
Look upon them as they slay 350
Till their rage has died away.

'Then they will return with shame
To the place from which they came,
And the blood thus shed will speak
In hot blushes on their cheek.

'Every woman in the land
Will point at them as they stand—
They will hardly dare to greet
Their acquaintance in the street.

'And the bold, true warriors 360
Who have hugged Danger in wars
Will turn to those who would be free,
Ashamed of such base company.

'And that slaughter to the Nation
Shall steam up like inspiration,
Eloquent, oracular;
A volcano heard afar.

'And these words shall then become
Like Oppression's thundered doom
Ringing through each heart and brain,   370
Heard again—again—again—

'Rise like Lions after slumber
In unvanquishable number—
Shake your chains to earth like dew
Which in sleep had fallen on you—
Ye are many—they are few.'

Peter Bell the Third

Part the Fifth

GRACE

Among the guests who often stayed
   Till the Devil's petits-soupers,
A man there came, fair as a maid,
And Peter noted what he said,
   Standing behind his master's chair

He was a mighty poet—and
   A subtle-souled psychologist;
All things he seemed to understand,
Of old or new—of sea or land—
   But his own mind—which was a mist

This was a man who might have turned
   Hell into Heaven—and so in gladness
A Heaven unto himself have earned;
But he in shadows undiscerned
   Trusted,—and damned himself to madness.

He spoke of poetry, and how
   'Divine it was—a light—a love—
A spirit which like wind doth blow
As it listeth, to and fro;
   A dew rained down from God above;

'A power which comes and goes like dream,
   And which none can ever trace—
Heaven's light on earth—Truth's brightest beam.'
And when he ceased there lay the gleam
   Of those words upon his face.

Now Peter, when he heard such talk,
   Would, heedless of a broken pate,
Stand like a man asleep, or balk
Some wishing guest of knife or fork,
   Or drop and break his master's plate.

At night he oft would start and wake
   Like a lover, and began
In a wild measure songs to make
On moor, and glen, and rocky lake,
   And on the heart of man—

And on the universal sky—
   And the wide earth's bosom green,—
And the sweet, strange mystery
Of what beyond these things may lie,
   And yet remain unseen.

For in his thought he visited
   The spots in which, ere dead and damned,
He his wayward life had led;
Yet knew not whence the thoughts were fed
   Which thus his fancy crammed.

And these obscure remembrances
    Stirred such harmony in Peter,
That, whensoever he should please,
He could speak of rocks and trees
    In poetic metre.

For though it was without a sense
    Of memory, yet he remembered well
Many a ditch and quick-set fence;
Of lakes he had intelligence,
    He knew something of heath and fell.

He had also dim recollections
    Of pedlars tramping on their rounds;
Milk-pans and pails; and odd collections
    Old parsons make in burying-grounds.

But Peter's verse was clear, and came
    Announcing from the frozen hearth
Of a cold age, that none might tame
The soul of that diviner flame
    It augured to the Earth:

Like gentle rains, on the dry plains,
    Making that green which late was gray,
Or like the sudden moon, that stains
Some gloomy chamber's window-panes
    With a broad light like day.

For language was in Peter's hand
    Like clay while he was yet a potter;
And he made songs for all the land,
Sweet both to feel and understand,
    As pipkins late to mountain Cotter.

And Mr. ——, the bookseller,
   Gave twenty pounds for some;—then scorning
A footman's yellow coat to wear,
Peter, too proud of heart, I fear,
   Instantly gave the Devil warning.

Whereat the Devil took offence,
   And swore in his soul a great oath then,
'That for his damned impertinence
He'd bring him to a proper sense
   Of what was due to gentlemen!'

Hellas

The Final Chorus

The world's great age begins anew,
   The golden years return,
The earth doth like a snake renew
   Her winter weeds outworn:
Heaven smiles, and faiths and empires gleam,
Like wrecks of a dissolving dream.

A brighter Hellas rears its mountains
   From waves serener far;
A new Peneus rolls his fountains
   Against the morning star.
Where fairer Tempes bloom, there sleep
Young Cyclads on a sunnier deep.

A loftier Argo cleaves the main,
   Fraught with a later prize;
Another Orpheus sings again,
   And loves, and weeps, and dies.
A new Ulysses leaves once more
Calypso for his native shore.

Oh, write no more the tale of Troy,
   If earth Death's scroll must be!
Nor mix with Laian rage the joy
   Which dawns upon the free:
Although a subtler Sphinx renew
Riddles of death Thebes never knew.

Another Athens shall arise,
   And to remoter time
Bequeath, like sunset to the skies,
   The splendour of its prime;
And leave, if nought so bright may live,
All earth can take or Heaven can give.

Saturn and Love their long repose
   Shall burst, more bright and good
Than all who fell, than One who rose,
   Than many unsubdued:
Not gold, not blood, their altar dowers,
But votive tears and symbol flowers.

Oh, cease! must hate and death return?
   Cease! must men kill and die?
Cease! drain not its dregs the urn
   Of bitter prophecy.
The world is weary of the past,
Oh, might it die or rest at last!

Ozymandias

I met a traveller from an antique land
Who said: Two vast and trunkless legs of stone
Stand in the desert . . . Near them, on the sand,
Half sunk, a shattered visage lies, whose frown,
And wrinkled lip, and sneer of cold command,
Tell that its sculptor well those passions read
Which yet survive, stamped on these lifeless things,
The hand that mocked them, and the heart that fed
And on the pedestal these words appear:
'My name is Ozymandias, king of kings:
Look on my works, ye Mighty, and despair!'
Nothing beside remains. Round the decay
Of that colossal wreck, boundless and bare
The lone and level sands stretch far away.

Song

Rarely, rarely, comest thou,
　　Spirit of Delight!
Wherefore hast thou left me now
　　Many a day and night?
Many a weary night and day
'Tis since thou art fled away.

How shall ever one like me
   Win thee back again?
With the joyous and the free
   Thou wilt scoff at pain.
Spirit false! thou hast forgot
All but those who need thee not.

As a lizard with the shade
   Of a trembling leaf,
Thou with sorrow art dismayed;
   Even the sighs of grief
Reproach thee, that thou art not near,
And reproach thou wilt not hear.

Let me set my mournful ditty
   To a merry measure;
Thou wilt never come for pity,
   Thou wilt come for pleasure;
Pity then will cut away
Those cruel wings, and thou wilt stay.

I love all that thou lovest,
   Spirit of Delight!
The fresh Earth in new leaves dressed,
   And the starry night;
Autumn evening, and the morn
When the golden mists are born.

I love snow, and all the forms
   Of the radiant frost;
I love waves, and winds, and storms,
   Everything almost
Which is Nature's, and may be
Untainted by man's misery.

I love tranquil solitude,
    And such society
As is quiet, wise, and good;
    Between thee and me
What difference? but thou dost possess
The things I seek, not love them less.

I love Love—though he has wings,
    And like light can flee,
But above all other things,
    Spirit, I love thee—
Thou art love and life! Oh, come,
Make once more my heart thy home.

The Indian Serenade

I arise from dreams of thee
In the first sweet sleep of night,
When the winds are breathing low,
And the stars are shining bright:
I arise from dreams of thee,
And a spirit in my feet
Hath led me—who knows how?
To thy chamber window, Sweet!

The wandering airs they faint
On the dark, the silent stream—
The Champak odours fail
Like sweet thoughts in a dream;
The nightingale's complaint,

It dies upon her heart;—
As I must on thine,
Oh, belovèd as thou art!

Oh, lirt me from the grass!
I die! I faint! I fail!
Let thy love in kisses rain
On my lips and eyelids pale.
My cheek is cold and white, alas!
My heart beats loud and fast;—
Oh! press it to thine own again,
Where it will break at last.

To Sophia

Thou art fair, and few are fairer
  Of the Nymphs of earth or ocean;
They are robes that fit the wearer—
  Those soft limbs of thine, whose motion
Ever falls and shifts and glances
As the life within them dances.

Thy deep eyes, a double Planet,
  Gaze the wisest into madness
With soft clear fire,—the winds that fan it
  Are those thoughts of tender gladness
Which, like zephyrs on the billow,
Make thy gentle soul their pillow.

If, whatever face thou paintest
  In those eyes, grows pale with pleasure,

If the fainting soul is faintest
   When it hears thy harp's wild measure,
Wonder not that when thou speakest
Of the weak my heart is weakest.

As dew beneath the wind of morning,
   As the sea which whirlwinds waken,
As the birds at thunder's warning,
   As aught mute yet deeply shaken,
As one who feels an unseen spirit
Is my heart when thine is near it.

To ——

I fear thy kisses, gentle maiden,
   Thou needest not fear mine;
My spirit is too deeply laden
   Ever to burthen thine.

I fear thy mien, thy tones, thy motion,
   Thou needest not fear mine;
Innocent is the heart's devotion
   With which I worship thine.

To Jane

The keen stars were twinkling,
And the fair moon was rising among them,
   Dear Jane!
   The guitar was tinkling,
But the notes were not sweet till you sung them
   Again.

As the moon's soft splendour
O'er the faint cold starlight of Heaven
    Is thrown,
    So your voice most tender
To the strings without soul had then given
    Its own.

The stars will awaken,
Though the moon sleep a full hour later,
    To-night;
    No leaf will be shaken
Whilst the dews of your melody scatter
    Delight.

Though the sound overpowers,
Sing again, with your dear voice revealing
    A tone
Of some world far from ours,
Where music and moonlight and feeling
    Are one.

To ——

One word is too often profaned
    For me to profane it,
One feeling too falsely disdained
    For thee to disdain it;
One hope is too like despair
    For prudence to smother,
And pity from thee more dear
    Than that from another.

I can give not what men call love,
But wilt thou accept not
The worship the heart lifts above
And the Heavens reject not,—
The desire of the moth for the star,
Of the night for the morrow,
The devotion to something afar
From the sphere of our sorrow?

An Exhortation

Chameleons feed on light and air:
Poet's food is love and fame:
If in this wide world of care
Poets could but find the same
With as little toil as they,
Would they ever change their hue
As the light chameleons do,
Suiting it to every ray
Twenty times a day?

Poets are on this cold earth,
As chameleons might be,
Hidden from their early birth
In a cave beneath the sea;
Where light is, chameleons change:
Where love is not, poets do:
Fame is love disguised: if few
Find either, never think it strange
That poets range.

Yet dare not stain with wealth or power
    A poet's free and heavenly mind:
If bright chameleons should devour
    Any food but beams and wind,
They would grow as earthly soon
    As their brother lizards are.
    Children of a sunnier star,
Spirits from beyond the moon,
        Oh, refuse the boon!

To a Skylark

Hail to thee, blithe Spirit!
    Bird thou never wert,
That from Heaven, or near it,
    Pourest thy full heart
In profuse strains of unpremeditated art.

Higher still and higher
    From the earth thou springest
Like a cloud of fire;
    The blue deep thou wingest,
And singing still dost soar, and soaring ever singest.   10

In the golden lightning
    Of the sunken sun,
O'er which clouds are bright'ning,
    Thou dost float and run;
Like an unbodied joy whose race is just begun.

The pale purple even
   Melts around thy flight;
Like a star of Heaven,
   In the broad daylight
Thou art unseen, but yet I hear thy shrill delight,   20

Keen as are the arrows
   Of that silver sphere,
Whose intense lamp narrows
   In the white dawn clear
Until we hardly see—we feel that it is there.

All the earth and air
   With thy voice is loud,
As, when night is bare,
   From one lonely cloud
The moon rains out her beams, and Heaven is overflowed.   30

What thou art we know not;
   What is most like thee?
From rainbow clouds there flow not
   Drops so bright to see
As from thy presence showers a rain of melody.

Like a Poet hidden
   In the light of thought,
Singing hymns unbidden,
   Till the world is wrought
To sympathy with hopes and fears it heeded not: 40

Like a high-born maiden
   In a palace-tower,
Soothing her love-laden
   Soul in secret hour
With music sweet as love, which overflows her bower:

Like a glow-worm golden
    In a dell of dew,
Scattering unbeholden
    Its aëreal hue
Among the flowers and grass, which screen it from the view! 50

Like a rose embowered
    In its own green leaves,
By warm winds deflowered,
    Till the scent it gives
Makes faint with too much sweet those heavy-wingèd thieves:

Sound of vernal showers
    On the twinkling grass,
Rain-awakened flowers,
    All that ever was
Joyous, and clear, and fresh, thy music doth surpass: 60

Teach us, Sprite or Bird,
    What sweet thoughts are thine:
I have never heard
    Praise of love or wine
That panted forth a flood of rapture so divine.

Chorus Hymeneal,
    Or triumphal chant,
Matched with thine would be all
    But an empty vaunt,
A thing wherein we feel there is some hidden want. 70

What objects are the fountains
    Of thy happy strain?
What fields, or waves, or mountains?
    What shapes of sky or plain?
What love of thine own kind? what ignorance of pain?

45

With thy clear keen joyance
  Languor cannot be:
Shadow of annoyance
  Never came near thee:
Thou lovest—but ne'er knew love's sad satiety.   80

Waking or asleep,
  Thou of death must deem
Things more true and deep
  Than we mortals dream,
Or how could thy notes flow in such a crystal stream?

We look before and after,
  And pine for what is not:
Our sincerest laughter
  With some pain is fraught;
Our sweetest songs are those that tell of saddest thought.   90

Yet if we could scorn
  Hate, and pride, and fear;
If we were things born
  Not to shed a tear,
I know not how thy joy we ever should come near.

Better than all measures
  Of delightful sound,
Better than all treasures
  That in books are found,
Thy skill to poet were, thou scorner of the ground!   100

Teach me half the gladness
  That thy brain must know,
Such harmonious madness
  From my lips would flow
The world should listen then—as I am listening now

The Question

I dreamed that, as I wandered by the way,
  Bare Winter suddenly was changed to Spring.
And gentle odours led my steps astray,
  Mixed with a sound of waters murmuring
Along a shelving bank of turf, which lay
  Under a copse, and hardly dared to fling
Its green arms round the bosom of the stream,
But kissed it and then fled, as thou mightest in dream.

There grew pied wind-flowers and violets,
  Daisies, those pearled Arcturi of the earth,   10
The constellated flower that never sets;
  Faint oxslips; tender bluebells, at whose birth
The sod scarce heaved; and that tall flower that wets—
  Like a child, half in tenderness and mirth—
Its mother's face with Heaven's collected tears,
When the low wind, its playmate's voice, it hears.

And in the warm hedge grew lush eglantine,
  Green cowbind and the moonlight-coloured may,
And cherry-blossoms, and white cups, whose wine
  Was the bright dew, yet drained not by day;   20
And wild roses, and ivy serpentine,
  With its dark buds and leaves, wandering astray;
And flowers azure, black, and streaked with gold,
Fairer than any wakened eyes behold.

And nearer to the river's trembling edge
  There grew broad flag-flowers, purple pranked with white,
And starry river buds among the sedge,
  And floating water-lilies, broad and bright,

47

Which lit the oak that overhung the hedge
  With moonlight beams of their own watery light;   30
And bulrushes, and reeds of such deep green
As soothed the dazzled eye with sober sheen.

Methought that of these visionary flowers
  I made a nosegay, bound in such a way
That the same hues, which in their natural bowers
  Were mingled or opposed, the like array
Kept these imprisoned children of the Hours
  Within my hand,—and then, elate and gay,
I hastened to the spot whence I had come,
That I might there present it!—Oh! to whom?   40

Ode to the West Wind

O wild West Wind, thou breath of Autumn's being,
Thou, from whose unseen presence the leaves dead
Are driven, like ghosts from an enchanter fleeing,

Yellow, and black, and pale, and hectic red,
Pestilence-stricken multitudes: O thou,
Who chariotest to their dark wintry bed

The wingèd seeds, where they lie cold and low,
Each like a corpse within its grave, until
Thine azure sister of the Spring shall blow

Her clarion o'er the dreaming earth, and fill   10
(Driving sweet buds like flocks to feed in air)
With living hues and odours plain and hill:

Wild Spirit, which art moving everywhere;
Destroyer and preserver; hear, oh, hear!

Thou on whose stream, mid the steep sky's commotion,
Loose clouds like earth's decaying leaves are shed,
Shook from the tangled boughs of Heaven and Ocean,

Angels of rain and lightning: there are spread
On the blue surface of thine aëry surge,
Like the bright hair uplifted from the head   20

Of some fierce Maenad, even from the dim verge
Of the horizon to the zenith's height,
The locks of the approaching storm. Thou dirge

Of the dying year, to which this closing night
Will be the dome of a vast sepulchre,
Vaulted with all thy congregated might

Of vapours, from whose solid atmosphere
Black rain, and fire, and hail will burst: oh, hear!

Thou who didst waken from his summer dreams
The blue Mediterranean, where he lay,   30
Lulled by the coil of his crystalline streams,

Beside a pumice isle in Baiae's bay,
And saw in sleep old palaces and towers
Quivering within the wave's intenser day,

All overgrown with azure moss and flowers
So sweet, the sense faints picturing them! Thou
For whose path the Atlantic's level powers

Cleave themselves into chasms, while far below
The sea-blooms and the oozy woods which wear
The sapless foliage of the ocean, know   40

Thy voice, and suddenly grow gray with fear,
And tremble and despoil themselves: oh, hear!

If I were a dead leaf thou mightest bear;
If I were a swift cloud to fly with thee;
A wave to pant beneath thy power, and share

The impulse of thy strength, only less free
Than thou, O uncontrollable! If even
I were as in my boyhood, and could be

The comrade of thy wanderings over Heaven,
As then, when to outstrip thy skiey speed   50
Scarce seemed a vision; I would ne'er have striven

As thus with thee in prayer in my sore need.
Oh, lift me as a wave, a leaf, a cloud!
I fall upon the thorns of life! I bleed!

A heavy weight of hours has chained and bowed
One too like thee: tameless, and swift, and proud

Make me thy lyre, even as the forest is:
What if my leaves are falling like its own!
The tumult of thy mighty harmonies

Will take from both a deep, autumnal tone,   60
Sweet though in sadness. Be thou, Spirit fierce,
My spirit! Be thou me, impetuous one!

Drive my dead thoughts over the universe
Like withered leaves to quicken a new birth!
And, by the incantation of this verse,

Scatter, as from an unextinguished hearth
Ashes and sparks, my words among mankind!
Be through my lips to unawakened earth

The trumpet of a prophecy! O, Wind,
If Winter comes, can Spring be far behind?   70

Hymn of Apollo

The sleepless Hours who watch me as I lie,
   Curtained with star-inwoven tapestries
From the broad moonlight of the sky,
   Fanning the busy dreams from my dim eyes,—
Waken me when their Mother, the gray Dawn,
Tells them that dreams and that the moon is gone.

Then I arise, and climbing Heaven's blue dome,
   I walk over the mountains and the waves,
Leaving my robe upon the ocean foam;
   My footsteps pave the clouds with fire; the caves   10
Are filled with my bright presence, and the air
Leaves the green Earth to my embraces bare.

The sunbeams are my shafts, with which I kill
   Deceit, that loves the night and fears the day:
All men who do or even imagine ill
   Fly me, and from the glory of my ray
Good minds and open actions take new might,
Until diminished by the reign of Night.

I feed the clouds, the rainbows and the flowers
   With their aethereal colours; the moon's globe   20
And the pure stars in their eternal bowers
   Are cinctured with my power as with a robe;
Whatever lamps on Earth or Heaven may shine
Are portions of one power, which is mine.

I stand at noon upon the peak of Heaven,
  Then with unwilling steps I wander down
Into the clouds of the Atlantic even;
  For grief that I depart they weep and frown:
What look is more delightful than the smile
With which I soothe them from the western isle?   30

I am the eye with which the Universe
  Beholds itself and knows itself divine;
All harmony of instrument or verse,
  All prophecy, all medicine is mine,
All light of art or nature;—to my song
Victory and praise in its own right belong.

The Cloud

I bring fresh showers for the thirsting flowers,
  From the seas and the streams;
I bear light shade for the leaves when laid
  In their noonday dreams.
From my wings are shaken the dews that waken
  The sweet buds every one,
When rocked to rest on their mother's breast,
  As she dances about the sun.
I wield the flail of the lashing hail,
  And whiten the green plains under,   10
And then again I dissolve it in rain,
  And laugh as I pass in thunder.

I sift the snow on the mountains below,
  And their great pines grown aghast;

And all the night 'tis my pillow white,
　　While I sleep in the arms of the blast.
Sublime on the towers of my skiey bowers,
　　Lightning my pilot sits;
In a cavern under is fettered the thunder,
　　It struggles and howls at fits;　　　　　　　20
Over earth and ocean, with gentle motion,
　　This pilot is guiding me,
Lured by the love of the genii that move
　　In the depths of the purple sea;
Over the rills, and the crags, and the hills,
　　Over the lakes and the plains,
Wherever he dream, under mountain or stream,
　　The Spirit he loves remains;
And I all the while bask in Heaven's blue smile,
　　Whilst he is dissolving in rains.　　　　　　30

The sanguine Sunrise, with his meteor eyes,
　　And his burning plumes outspread,
Leaps on the back of my sailing rack,
　　When the morning star shines dead;
As on the jag of a mountain crag,
　　Which an earthquake rocks and swings,
An eagle alit one moment may sit
　　In the light of its golden wings.
And when Sunset may breathe, from the lit sea beneath,
　　Its ardours of rest and of love,　　　　　　40
And the crimson pall of eve may fall
　　From the depth of Heaven above,
With wings folded I rest, on mine aëry nest,
　　As still as a brooding dove.

That orbèd maiden with white fire laden,
　　Whom mortals call the Moon,

Glides glimmering o'er my fleece-like floor,
    By the midnight breezes strewn;
And wherever the beat of her unseen feet,
    Which only the angels hear,   50
May have broken the woof of my tent's thin roof,
    The stars peep behind her and peer;
And I laugh to see them whirl and flee,
    Like a swarm of golden bees,
When I widen the rent in my wind-built tent,
    Till the calm rivers, lakes, and seas,
Like strips of the sky fallen through me on high,
    Are each paved with the moon and these.

I bind the Sun's throne with a burning zone,
    And the Moon's with a girdle of pearl;   60
The volcanoes are dim, and the stars reel and swim,
    When the whirlwinds my banner unfurl.
From cape to cape, with a bridge-like shape,
    Over a torrent sea,
Sunbeam-proof, I hang like a roof,—
    The mountains its columns be.
The triumphal arch through which I march
    With hurricane, fire, and snow,
When the powers of the air are chained to my chair,
    Is the million-coloured bow;   70
The sphere-fire above its soft colours wove,
    While the moist earth was laughing below.

I am the daughter of Earth and Water,
    And the nursling of the Sky;
I pass through the pores of the ocean and shores;
    I change but I cannot die.
For after the rain when with never a stain
    The pavilion of Heaven is bare,

And the winds and sunbeams with their convex gleams
    Build up the blue dome of air,   80
I silently laugh at my own cenotaph,
    And out of the caverns of rain,
Like a child from the womb, like a ghost from the tomb,
    I arise and unbuild it again.

Ode to Heaven

Chorus of Spirits

FIRST SPIRIT

Palace-roof of cloudless nights!
Paradise of golden lights!
    Deep, immeasurable, vast,
Which art now, and which wert then
    Of the Present and the Past,
Of the eternal Where and When,
    Presence-chamber, temple, home,
    Ever-canopying dome,
    Of acts and ages yet to come!

Glorious shapes have life in thee,   10
Earth, and all earth's company;
    Living globes which ever throng
Thy deep chasms and wildernesses;
    And green worlds that glide along;
And swift stars with flashing tresses;
    And icy moons most cold and bright,
    And mighty suns beyond the night,
    Atoms of intensest light.

Even thy name is as a god,
Heaven! for thou art the abode   20
  Of that Power which is the glass
Wherein man his nature sees.
  Generations as they pass
Worship thee with bended knees.
  Their unremaining gods and they
  Like a river roll away:
  Thou remainest such—alway!—

SECOND SPIRIT

Thou art but the mind's first chamber,
Round which its young fancies clamber,
  Like weak insects in a cave,   30
Lighted up by stalactites;
  But the portal of the grave,
Where a world of new delights
  Will make thy best glories seem
  But a dim and noonday gleam
  From the shadow of a dream!

THIRD SPIRIT

Peace! the abyss is wreathed with scorn
At your presumption, atom-born!
  What is Heaven? and what are ye
Who its brief expanse inherit?   40
  What are suns and spheres which flee
With the instinct of that Spirit
  Of which ye are but a part?
  Drops which Nature's mighty heart
  Drives through thinnest veins! Depart!

56

What is Heaven? a globe of dew,
Filling in the morning new
  Some eyed flower whose young leaves waken
On an unimagined world:
  Constellated suns unshaken,   50
Orbits measureless, are furled
  In that frail and fading sphere,
  With ten millions gathered there,
  To tremble, gleam, and disappear.

Adonais

I weep for Adonais—he is dead!
O, weep for Adonais! though our tears
Thaw not the frost which binds so dear a head!
And thou, sad Hour, selected from all years
To mourn our loss, rouse thy obscure compeers,
And teach them thine own sorrow, say: 'With me
Died Adonais; till the Future dares
Forget the Past, his fate and fame shall be
An echo and a light unto eternity!'

Where wert thou, mighty Mother, when he lay,   10
When thy Son lay, pierced by the shaft which flies
In darkness? where was lorn Urania
When Adonais died? With veilèd eyes,
'Mid listening Echoes, in her Paradise
She sate, while one, with soft enamoured breath,
Rekindled all the fading melodies,
With which, like flowers that mock the corse beneath,
He had adorned and hid the coming bulk of Death.

Oh, weep for Adonais—he is dead!
Wake, melancholy Mother, wake and weep! 20
Yet wherefore? Quench within their burning bed
Thy fiery tears, and let thy loud heart keep
Like his, a mute and uncomplaining sleep;
For he is gone, where all things wise and fair
Descend;—oh, dream not that the amorous Deep
Will yet restore him to the vital air;
Death feeds on his mute voice, and laughs at our despair.

Most musical of mourners, weep again!
Lament anew, Urania!—He died,
Who was the Sire of an immortal strain, 30
Blind, old, and lonely, when his country's pride,
The priest, the slave, and the liberticide,
Trampled and mocked with many a loathèd rite
Of lust and blood; he went, unterrified,
Into the gulf of death; but his clear Sprite
Yet reigns o'er earth; the third among the sons of light.

Most musical of mourners, weep anew!
Not all to that bright station dared to climb;
And happier they their happiness who knew,
Whose tapers yet burn through that night of time 40
In which suns perished; others more sublime,
Struck by the envious wrath of man or god,
Have sunk, extinct in their refulgent prime;
And some yet live, treading the thorny road,
Which leads, through toil and hate, to Fame's serene abode.

But now, thy youngest, dearest one, has perished—
The nursling of thy widowhood, who grew,
Like a pale flower by some sad maiden cherished,
And fed with true-love tears, instead of dew;

Most musical of mourners, weep anew! 50
Thy extreme hope, the loveliest and the last.
The bloom, whose petals nipped before they blew
Died on the promise of the fruit, is waste;
The broken lily lies—the storm is overpast.

To that high Capital, where kingly Death
Keeps his pale court in beauty and decay,
He came; and bought, with price of purest breath,
A grave among the eternal.—Come away!
Haste, while the vault of blue Italian day
Is yet his fitting charnel-roof! while still 60
He lies, as if in dewy sleep he lay;
Awake him not! surely he takes his fill
Of deep and liquid rest, forgetful of all ill.

He will awake no more, oh, never more!—
Within the twilight chamber spreads apace
The shadow of white Death, and at the door
Invisible Corruption waits to trace
His extreme way to her dim dwelling-place;
The eternal Hunger sits, but pity and awe
Soothe her pale rage, nor dares she to deface 70
So fair a prey, till darkness, and the law
Of change shall o'er his sleep the mortal curtain draw.

Oh, weep for Adonais!—The quick Dreams,
The passion-wingèd Ministers of thought,
Who were his flocks, whom near the living streams
Of his young spirit he fed, and whom he taught
The love which was its music, wander not,—
Wander no more, from kindling brain to brain,
But droop there, whence they sprung; and mourn their lot
Round the cold heart, where, after their sweet pain, 80
They ne'er will gather strength, or find a home again.

And one with trembling hands clasps his cold head,
And fans him with her moonlight wings, and cries;
'Our love, our hope, our sorrow, is not dead;
See, on the silken fringe of his faint eyes,
Like dew upon a sleeping flower, there lies
A tear some Dream has loosened from his brain.'
Lost Angel of a ruined Paradise!
She knew not 'twas her own; as with no stain
She faded, like a cloud which had outwept its rain.   90

One from a lucid urn of starry dew
Washed his light limbs as if embalming them;
Another clipped her profuse locks, and threw
The wreath upon him, like an anadem,
Which frozen tears instead of pearls begem;
Another in her wilful grief would break
Her bow and wingèd reeds, as if to stem
A greater loss with one which was more weak;
And dull the barbèd fire against his frozen cheek.

Another Splendour on his mouth alit,   100
That mouth, whence it was wont to draw the breath
Which gave it strength to pierce the guarded wit,
And pass into the panting heart beneath
With lightning and with music: the damp death
Quenched its caress upon his icy lips;
And, as a dying meteor stains a wreath
Of moonlight vapour, which the cold night clips,
It flushed through his pale limbs, and passed to its eclipse.

And others came . . . Desires and Adorations,
Wingèd Persuasions and veiled Destinies,   110
Splendours, and Glooms, and glimmering Incarnations
Of hopes and fears, and twilight Phantasies;

And Sorrow, with her family of Sighs,
And Pleasure, blind with tears, led by the gleam
Of her own dying smile instead of eyes,
Came in slow pomp;—the moving pomp might seem
Like pageantry of mist on an autumnal stream.

All he had loved, and moulded into thought,
From shape, and hue, and odour, and sweet sound,
Lamented Adonais. Morning sought   120
Her eastern watch-tower, and her hair unbound,
Wet with the tears which should adorn the ground,
Dimmed the aëreal eyes that kindle day;
Afar the melancholy thunder moaned,
Pale Ocean in unquiet slumber lay,
And the wild Winds flew round, sobbing in their dismay.

Lost Echo sits amid the voiceless mountains,
And feeds her grief with his remembered lay,
And will no more reply to winds or fountains,
Or amorous birds perched on the young green spray,   130
Or herdsman's horn, or bell at closing day;
Since she can mimic not his lips, more dear
Than those for whose disdain she pined away
Into a shadow of all sounds:—a drear
Murmur, between their songs, is all the woodmen hear.

Grief made the young Spring wild, and she threw down
Her kindling buds, as if she Autumn were,
Or they dead leaves; since her delight is flown,
For whom should she have waked the sullen year?
To Phoebus was not Hyacinth so dear   140
Nor to himself Narcissus, as to both
Thou, Adonais: wan they stand and sere
Amid the faint companions of their youth,
With dew all turned to tears; odour, to sighing ruth.

Thy spirit's sister, the lorn nightingale
Mourns not her mate with such melodious pain;
Not so the eagle, who like thee could scale
Heaven, and could nourish in the sun's domain
Her mighty youth with morning, doth complain,
Soaring and screaming round her empty nest,   150
As Albion wails for thee: the curse of Cain
Light on his head who pierced thy innocent breast,
And scared the angel soul that was its earthly guest!

Ah, woe is me! Winter is come and gone,
But grief returns with the revolving year;
The airs and streams renew their joyous tone;
The ants, the bees, the swallows reappear;
Fresh leaves and flowers deck the dead Season's bier;
The amorous birds now pair in every brake,
And build their mossy homes in field and brere;   160
And the green lizard, and the golden snake,
Like unimprisoned flames, out of their trance awake.

Through wood and stream and field and hill and Ocean
A quickening life from the Earth's heart has burst
As it has ever done, with change and motion,
From the great morning of the world when first
God dawned on Chaos; in its stream immersed,
The lamps of Heaven flash with a softer light;
All baser things pant with life's sacred thirst;
Diffuse themselves; and spend in love's delight,   170
The beauty and the joy of their renewèd might.

The leprous corpse, touched by this spirit tender,
Exhales itself in flowers of gentle breath;
Like incarnations of the stars, when splendour
Is changed to fragrance, they illumine death

And mock the merry worm that wakes beneath;
Nought we know, dies. Shall that alone which knows
Be as a sword consumed before the sheath
By sightless lightning?—the intense atom glows
A moment, then is quenched in a most cold repose.　　　180

Alas! that all we loved of him should be,
But for our grief, as if it had not been,
And grief itself be mortal! Woe is me!
Whence are we, and why are we? of what scene
The actors or spectators? Great and mean
Meet massed in death, who lends what life must borrow.
As long as skies are blue, and fields are green,
Evening must usher night, night urge the morrow,
Month follow month with woe, and year wake year to sorrow.

He will awake no more, oh, never more!　　　190
'Wake thou,' cried Misery, 'childless Mother, rise
Out of thy sleep, and slake, in thy heart's core,
A wound more fierce than his, with tears and sighs.'
And all the Dreams that watched Urania's eyes,
And all the Echoes whom their sister's song
Had held in holy silence, cried: 'Arise!'
Swift as a Thought by the snake Memory stung,
From her ambrosial rest the fading Splendour sprung.

She rose like an autumnal Night, that springs
Out of the East, and follows wild and drear　　　200
The golden Day, which, on eternal wings,
Even as a ghost abandoning a bier,
Had left the Earth a corpse. Sorrow and fear
So struck, so roused, so rapt Urania;
So saddened round her like an atmosphere
Of stormy mist; so swept her on her way
Even to the mournful place where Adonais lay.

63

Out of her secret Paradise she sped,
Through camps and cities rough with stone, and steel,
And human hearts, which to her aery tread   210
Yielding not, wounded the invisible
Palms of her tender feet where'er they fell:
And barbèd tongues, and thoughts more sharp than they,
Rent the soft Form they never could repel,
Whose sacred blood, like the young tears of May,
Paved with eternal flowers that undeserving way.

In the death-chamber for a moment Death,
Shamed by the presence of that living Might,
Blushed to annihilation, and the breath
Revisited those lips, and Life's pale light   220
Flashed through those limbs, so late her dear delight.
'Leave me not wild and drear and comfortless,
As silent lightning leaves the starless night!
Leave me not!' cried Urania: her distress
Roused Death: Death rose and smiled, and met her vain caress.

'Stay yet awhile! speak to me once again;
Kiss me, so long but as a kiss may live;
And in my heartless breast and burning brain
That word, that kiss, shall all thoughts else survive,
With food of saddest memory kept alive,   230
Now thou art dead, as if it were a part
Of thee, my Adonais! I would give
All that I am to be as thou now art!
But I am chained to Time, and cannot thence depart!

'O gentle child, beautiful as thou wert,
Why didst thou leave the trodden paths of men
Too soon, and with weak hands though mighty heart
Dare the unpastured dragon in his den?

Defenceless as thou wert, oh, where was then
Wisdom the mirrored shield, or scorn the spear?   240
Or hadst thou waited the full cycle, when
Thy spirit should have filled its crescent sphere,
The monsters of life's waste had fled from thee like deer.

'The herded wolves, bold only to pursue;
The obscene ravens, clamorous o'er the dead;
The vultures to the conqueror's banner true
Who feed where Desolation first has fed,
And whose wings rain contagion;—how they fled,
When, like Apollo, from his golden bow
The Pythian of the age one arrow sped   250
And smiled!—The spoilers tempt no second blow,
They fawn on the proud feet that spurn them lying low.

'The sun comes forth, and many reptiles spawn;
He sets, and each ephemeral insect then
Is gathered into death without a dawn,
And the immortal stars awake again;
So is it in the world of living men:
A godlike mind soars forth, in its delight
Making earth bare and veiling heaven, and when
It sinks, the swarms that dimmed or shared its light   260
Leave to its kindred lamps the spirit's awful night.'

Thus ceased she: and the mountain shepherds came,
Their garlands sere, their magic mantles rent;
The Pilgrim of Eternity, whose fame
Over his living head like Heaven is bent,
An early but enduring monument,
Came, veiling all the lightnings of his song
In sorrow; from her wilds Ierne sent
The sweetest lyrist of her saddest wrong,
And Love taught Grief to fall like music from his tongue.   270

Midst others of less note, came one frail Form,
A phantom among men; companionless
As the last cloud of an expiring storm
Whose thunder is its knell; he, as I guess,
Had gazed on Nature's naked loveliness,
Actaeon-like, and now he fled astray
With feeble steps o'er the world's wilderness,
And his own thoughts, along that rugged way,
Pursued, like raging hounds, their father and their prey.

A pardlike Spirit beautiful and swift—   280
A Love in desolation masked;—a Power
Girt round with weakness;—it can scarce uplift
The weight of the superincumbent hour;
It is a dying lamp, a falling shower,
A breaking billow;—even whilst we speak
Is it not broken? On the withering flower
The killing sun smiles brightly: on a cheek
The life can burn in blood, even while the heart may break.

His head was bound with pansies overblown,
And faded violets, white, and pied, and blue;   290
And a light spear topped with a cypress cone,
Round whose rude shaft dark ivy-tresses grew
Yet dripping with the forest's noonday dew,
Vibrated, as the ever-beating heart
Shook the weak hand that grasped it; of that crew
He came the last, neglected and apart;
A herd-abandoned deer struck by the hunter's dart.

All stood aloof, and at his partial moan
Smiled through their tears; well knew that gentle band
Who in another's fate now wept his own,   300
As in the accents of an unknown land

He sung new sorrow; sad Urania scanned
The Stranger's mien, and murmured: 'Who art thou?'
He answered not, but with a sudden hand
Made bare his branded and ensanguined brow,
Which was like Cain's or Christ's—oh! that it should be so!

What softer voice is hushed over the dead?
Athwart what brow is that dark mantle thrown?
What form leans sadly o'er the white death-bed,
In mockery of monumental stone,   310
The heavy heart heaving without a moan?
If it be He, who, gentlest of the wise,
Taught, soothed, loved, honoured the departed one,
Let me not vex, with inharmonious sighs,
The silence of that heart's accepted sacrifice.

Our Adonais has drunk poison—oh!
What deaf and viperous murderer could crown
Life's early cup with such a draught of woe?
The nameless worm would now itself disown:
It felt, yet could escape, the magic tone   320
Whose prelude held all envy, hate, and wrong,
But what was howling in one breast alone,
Silent with expectation of the song,
Whose master's hand is cold, whose silver lyre unstrung.

Live thou, whose infamy is not thy fame!
Live! fear no heavier chastisement from me,
Thou noteless blot on a remembered name!
But be thyself, and know thyself to be!
And ever at thy season be thou free
To spill the venom when thy fangs o'erflow: 330
Remorse and Self-contempt shall cling to thee;
Hot Shame shall burn upon thy secret brow,
And like a beaten hound tremble thou shalt—as now.

Nor let us weep that our delight is fled
Far from these carrion kites that scream below;
He wakes or sleeps with the enduring dead;
Thou canst not soar where he is sitting now.—
Dust to the dust! but the pure spirit shall flow
Back to the burning fountain whence it came,
A portion of the Eternal, which must glow   340
Through time and change, unquenchably the same,
Whilst thy cold embers choke the sordid hearth of shame.

Peace, peace! he is not dead, he doth not sleep—
He hath awakened from the dream of life—
'Tis we, who lost in stormy visions, keep
With phantoms an unprofitable strife,
And in mad trance, strike with our spirit's knife
Invulnerable nothings.—*We* decay
Like corpses in a charnel; fear and grief
Convulse us and consume us day by day,   350
And cold hopes swarm like worms within our living clay.

He has outsoared the shadow of our night;
Envy and calumny and hate and pain,
And that unrest which men miscall delight,
Can touch him not and torture not again;
From the contagion of the world's slow stain
He is secure, and now can never mourn
A heart grown cold, a head grown gray in vain;
Nor, when the spirit's self has ceased to burn,
With sparkless ashes load an unlamented urn.   360

He lives, he wakes—'tis Death is dead, not he;
Mourn not for Adonais.—Thou young Dawn,
Turn all thy dew to splendour, for from thee
The spirit thou lamentest is not gone;

Ye caverns and ye forests, cease to moan!
Cease, ye faint flowers and fountains, and thou Air,
Which like a mourning veil thy scarf hadst thrown
O'er the abandoned Earth, now leave it bare
Even to the joyous stars which smile on its despair!

He is made one with Nature: there is heard   370
His voice in all her music, from the moan
Of thunder, to the song of night's sweet bird;
He is a presence to be felt and known
In darkness and in light, from herb and stone,
Spreading itself where'er that Power may move
Which has withdrawn his being to its own;
Which wields the world with never-wearied love,
Sustains it from beneath, and kindles it above.

He is a portion of the loveliness
Which once he made more lovely: he doth bear   380
His part, while the one Spirit's plastic stress
Sweeps through the dull dense world, compelling there,
All new successions to the forms they wear;
Torturing th' unwilling dross that checks its flight
To its own likeness, as each mass may bear;
And bursting in its beauty and its might
From trees and beasts and men into the Heaven's light.

The splendours of the firmament of time
May be eclipsed, but are extinguished not;
Like stars to their appointed height they climb,   390
And death is a low mist which cannot blot
The brightness it may veil. When lofty thought
Lifts a young heart above its mortal lair,
And love and life contend in it, for what
Shall be its earthly doom, the dead live there
And move like winds of light on dark and stormy air.

The inheritors of unfulfilled renown
Rose from their thrones, built beyond mortal thought,
Far in the Unapparent. Chatterton
Rose pale,—his solemn agony had not   400
Yet faded from him; Sidney, as he fought
And as he fell and as he lived and loved
Sublimely mild, a Spirit without spot,
Arose; and Lucan, by his death approved:
Oblivion as they rose shrank like a thing reproved.

And many more, whose names on Earth are dark,
But whose transmitted effluence cannot die
So long as fire outlives the parent spark,
Rose, robed in dazzling immortality.
'Thou art become as one of us,' they cry,   410
'It was for thee yon kingless sphere has long
Swung blind in unascended majesty,
Silent alone amid an Heaven of Song.
Assume thy wingèd throne, thou Vesper of our throng!'

Who mourns for Adonais? Oh, come forth,
Fond wretch! and know thyself and him aright.
Clasp with thy panting soul the pendulous Earth;
As from a centre, dart thy spirit's light
Beyond all worlds, until its spacious might
Satiate the void circumference: then shrink   420
Even to a point within our day and night;
And keep thy heart light lest it makes thee sink
When hope has kindled hope, and lured thee to the brink

Or go to Rome, which is the sepulchre,
Oh, not of him, but of our joy: 'tis nought
That ages, empires, and religions there
Lie buried in the ravage they have wrought;

For such as he can lend,—they borrow not
Glory from those who made the world their prey;
And he is gathered to the kings of thought   430
Who waged contention with their time's decay,
And of the past are all that cannot pass away.

Go thou to Rome,—at once the Paradise,
The grave, the city, and the wilderness;
And where its wrecks like shattered mountains rise,
And flowering weeds, and fragrant copses dress
The bones of Desolation's nakedness
Pass, till the spirit of the spot shall lead
Thy footsteps to a slope of green access
Where, like an infant's smile, over the dead   440
A light of laughing flowers along the grass is spread;

And gray walls moulder round, on which dull Time
Feeds, like slow fire upon a hoary brand;
And one keen pyramid with wedge sublime,
Pavilioning the dust of him who planned
This refuge for his memory, doth stand
Like flame transformed to marble; and beneath,
A field is spread, on which a newer band
Have pitched in Heaven's smile their camp of death,
Welcoming him we lose with scarce extinguished breath.   450

Here pause: these graves are all too young as yet
To have outgrown the sorrow which consigned
Its charge to each; and if the seal is set,
Here, on one fountain of a mourning mind,
Break it not thou! too surely shalt thou find
Thine own well full, if thou returnest home,
Of tears and gall. From the world's bitter wind
Seek shelter in the shadow of the tomb.
What Adonais is, why fear we to become?

The One remains, the many change and pass; 460
Heaven's light forever shines, Earth's shadows fly;
Life, like a dome of many-coloured glass,
Stains the white radiance of Eternity,
Until death tramples it to fragments.—Die,
If thou wouldst be with that which thou dost seek!
Follow where all is fled!—Rome's azure sky,
Flowers, ruins, statues, music, words, are weak
The glory they transfuse with fitting truth to speak.

Why linger, why turn back, why shrink, my Heart?
Thy hopes are gone before: from all things here 470
They have departed; thou shouldst now depart!
A light is passed from the revolving year,
And man, and woman; and what still is dear
Attracts to crush, repels to make thee wither,
The soft sky smiles,—the low wind whispers near:
'Tis Adonais calls! oh, hasten thither,
No more let Life divide what Death can join together.

That Light whose smile kindles the Universe,
That Beauty in which all things work and move,
That Benediction which the eclipsing Curse 480
Of birth can quench not, that sustaining Love
Which through the web of being blindly wove
By man and beast and earth and air and sea,
Burns bright or dim, as each are mirrors of
The fire for which all thirst; now beams on me,
Consuming the last clouds of cold mortality.

The breath whose might I have invoked in song
Descends on me; my spirit's bark is driven,
Far from the shore, far from the trembling throng
Whose sails were never to the tempest given; 490

The massy earth and spherèd skies are riven!
I am borne darkly, fearfully, afar;
Whilst, burning through the inmost veil of Heaven,
The soul of Adonais, like a star,
Beacons from the abode where the Eternal are.

From

The Witch of Atlas

. . . All day the wizard lady sate aloof,
    Spelling out scrolls of dread antiquity,
Under the cavern's fountain-lighted roof;
    Or broidering the pictured poesy
Of some high tale upon her growing woof,
    Which the sweet splendour of her smiles could dye
In hues outshining heaven—and ever she
Added some grace to the wrought poesy.

While on her hearth lay blazing many a piece
    Of sandal wood, rare gums, and cinnamon;
Men scarcely know how beautiful fire is—
    Each flame of it is as a precious stone
Dissolved in ever-moving light, and this
    Belongs to each and all who gaze upon.
The Witch beheld it not, for in her hand
She held a woof that dimmed the burning brand.

This lady never slept, but lay in trance
    All night within the fountain—as in sleep.
Its emerald crags glowed in her beauty's glance;
    Through the green splendour of the water deep

She saw the constellations reel and dance
  Like fire-flies—and withal did ever keep
The tenour of her contemplations calm,
With open eyes, closed feet, and folded palm.

And when the whirlwinds and the clouds descended
  From the white pinnacles of that cold hill,
She passed at dewfall to a space extended,
  Where in a lawn of flowering asphodel
Amid a wood of pines and cedars blended,
  There yawned an inextinguishable well
Of crimson fire—full even to the brim,
And overflowing all the margin trim.

Within the which she lay when the fierce war
  Of wintry winds shook that innocuous liquor
In many a mimic moon and bearded star
  O'er woods and lawns;—the serpent heard it flicker
In sleep, and dreaming still, he crept afar—
  And when the windless snow descended thicker
Than autumn leaves, she watched it as it came
Melt on the surface of the level flame.

She had a boat, which some say Vulcan wrought
  For Venus, as the chariot of her star;
But it was found too feeble to be fraught
  With all the ardours in that sphere which are,
And so she sold it, and Apollo bought
  And gave it to this daughter: from a car
Changed to the fairest and the lightest boat
Which ever upon mortal stream did float.

And others say, that, when but three hours old,
  The first-born Love out of his cradle lept,

And clove dun Chaos with his wings of gold,
    And like a horticultural adept,
Stole a strange seed, and wrapped it up in mould,
    And sowed it in his mother's star, and kept
Watering it all the summer with sweet dew,
And with his wings fanning it as it grew.

The plant grew strong and green, the snowy flower
    Fell, and the long and gourd-like fruit began
To turn the light and dew by inward power
    To its own substance; woven tracery ran
Of light firm texture, ribbed and branching, o'er
    The solid rind, like a leaf's veinèd fan—
Of which Love scooped this boat—and with soft motion
Piloted it round the circumfluous ocean.

Extracts from

Prometheus Unbound

*Act II, Scene II:—The descent of Asia and Panthea to the
Cave of Demogoroon.*

SEMICHORUS I OF SPIRITS

The path through which that lovely twain
    Have passed, by cedar, pine, and yew,
    And each dark tree that ever grew,
    Is curtained out from Heaven's wide blue;
Nor sun, nor moon, nor wind, nor rain,
        Can pierce its interwoven bowers,
    Nor aught, save where some cloud of dew,
Drifted along the earth-creeping breeze,
Between the trunks of the hoar trees,

Hangs each a pearl in the pale flowers
  Of the green laurel, blown anew;
And bends, and then fades silently,
One frail and fair anemone:
Or when some star of many a one
That climbs and wanders through steep night,
Has found the cleft through which alone
Beams fall from high those depths upon
Ere it is borne away, away,
By the swift Heavens that cannot stay,
It scatters drops of golden light,
Like lines of rain that ne'er unite:
And the gloom divine is all around,
And underneath is the mossy ground.

SEMICHORUS II

There the voluptuous nightingales,
  Are awake through all the broad noonday.
When one with bliss or sadness fails,
    And through the windless ivy-boughs,
  Sick with sweet love, droops dying away
On its mate's music-panting bosom;
Another from the swinging blossom, 30
    Watching to catch the languid close
  Of the last strain, then lifts on high
  The wings of the weak melody,
'Till some new strain of feeling bear
  The song, and all the woods are mute;
When there is heard through the dim air
The rush of wings, and rising there
  Like many a lake-surrounded flute,
Sounds overflow the listener's brain
So sweet, that joy is almost pain. 40

There those enchanted eddies play
  Of echoes, music-tongued, which draw,
  By Demogorgon's mighty law,
  With melting rapture, or sweet awe,
All spirits on that secret way;
  As inland boats are driven to Ocean
Down streams made strong with mountain-thaw:
    And first there comes a gentle sound
    To those in talk or slumber bound,
    And wakes the destined soft emotion,—   50
Attracts, impels them; those who saw
  Say from the breathing earth behind
  There steams a plume-uplifting wind
Which drives them on their path, while they
  Believe their own swift wings and feet
The sweet desires within obey:
And so they float upon their way,
Until, still sweet, but loud and strong,
The storm of sound is driven along,
  Sucked up and hurrying: as they fleet   60
  Behind, its gathering billows meet
And to the fatal mountain bear
Like clouds amid the yielding air.

From Act II, Scene V:—The Transformation of Asia.

VOICE IN THE AIR, SINGING

Life of Life! thy lips enkindle
  With their love the breath between them;

And thy smiles before they dwindle
　　Make the cold air fire; then screen them
In those looks, where whoso gazes
Faints, entangled in their mazes.

Child of Light! thy limbs are burning
　　Through the vest which seems to hide them;
As the radiant lines of morning
　　Through the clouds ere they divide them;　　10
And this atmosphere divinest
Shrouds thee wheresoe'er thou shinest.

Fair are others; none beholds thee,
　　But thy voice sounds low and tender
Like the fairest, for it folds thee
　　From the sight, that liquid splendour,
And all feel, yet see thee never,
As I feel now, lost for ever!

Lamp of Earth! where'er thou movest
　　Its dim shapes are clad with brightness,　　20
And the souls of whom thou lovest
　　Walk upon the winds with lightness,
Till they fail, as I am failing,
Dizzy, lost, yet unbewailing!

Act IV

SCENE.—*A Part of the Forest near the Cave of* PROMETHEUS. PANTHEA
and IONE *are sleeping: they awaken gradually during the first Song.*

VOICE OF UNSEEN SPIRITS

The pale stars are gone!
For the sun, their swift shepherd,

To their folds them compelling,
   In the depths of the dawn,
Hastes, in meteor-eclipsing array, and they flee
   Beyond his blue dwelling,
   As fawns flee the leopard.
      But where are ye?

A TRAIN OF DARK FORMS AND SHADOWS PASSES BY
CONFUSEDLY, SINGING

      Here, oh, here:
      We bear the bier   10
Of the Father of many a cancelled year!
      Spectres we
      Of the dead Hours be,
We bear Time to his tomb in eternity.

      Strew, oh, strew
      Hair, not yew!
Wet the dusty pall with tears, not dew!
      Be the faded flowers
      Of Death's bare bowers
Spread on the corpse of the King of Hours!   20

      Haste, oh, haste!
      As shades are chased,
Trembling, by day, from heaven's blue waste.
      We melt away,
      Like dissolving spray,
From the children of a diviner day,
      With the lullaby
      Of winds that die
On the bosom of their own harmony!

IONE

What dark forms were they?

PANTHEA

The past Hours weak and gray,
With the spoil which their toil
   Raked together
From the conquest but One could foil.

IONE

Have they passed?

PANTHEA

            They have passed;
They outspeeded the blast,
While 'tis said, they are fled:

IONE

Whither, oh, whither?

PANTHEA

To the dark, to the past, to the dead.

VOICE OF UNSEEN SPIRITS

Bright clouds float in heaven,
Dew-stars gleam on earth,
Waves assemble on ocean,
They are gathered and driven
By the storm of delight, by the panic of glee!
They shake with emotion,
They dance in their mirth.
   But where are ye?

The pine boughs are singing
Old songs with new gladness,
The billows and fountains   50
Fresh music are flinging,
Like the notes of a spirit from land and from sea;
The storms mock the mountains
With the thunder of gladness.
    But where are ye?

IONE   What charioteers are these?

PANTHEA   Where are their chariots?

SEMICHORUS OF HOURS
The voice of the Spirits of Air and of Earth
  Have drawn back the figured curtain of sleep
Which covered our being and darkened our birth
  In the deep.

A VOICE
In the deep?

SEMICHORUS II
                          Oh, below the deep.   60

SEMICHORUS I
An hundred ages we had been kept
  Cradled in visions of hate and care,
And each one who waked as his brother slept,
  Found the truth—

SEMICHORUS II
                    Worse than his visions were!

SEMICHORUS I
We have heard the lute of Hope in sleep;

We have known the voice of Love in dreams;
We have felt the wand of Power, and leap—

SEMICHORUS II
As the billows leap in the morning beams!

CHORUS
Weave the dance on the floor of the breeze,
    Pierce with song heaven's silent light, 70
Enchant the day that too swiftly flees,
    To check its flight ere the cave of Night.

Once the hungry Hours were hounds
    Which chased the day like a bleeding deer,
And it limped and stumbled with many wounds
    Through the nightly dells of the desert year.

But now, oh weave the mystic measure
    Of music, and dance, and shapes of light,
Let the Hours, and the spirits of might and pleasure,
    Like the clouds and sunbeams, unite.

A VOICE
        Unite! 80
PANTHEA See, where the Spirits of the human mind
Wrapped in sweet sounds, as in bright veils, approach.

CHORUS OF SPIRITS
    We join the throng
    Of the dance and the song,
  By the whirlwind of gladness borne along;
    As the flying fish leap
    From the Indian deep,
And mix with the sea-birds, half asleep.

Whence come ye, so wild and so fleet,
For sandals of lightning are on your feet,   90
And your wings are soft and swift as thought,
And your eyes are as love which is veilèd not?

CHORUS OF SPIRITS
    We come from the mind
    Of human kind
Which was late so dusk, and obscene, and blind,
    Now 'tis an ocean
    Of clear emotion,
A heaven of serene and mighty motion

    From that deep abyss
    Of wonder and bliss,   100
Whose caverns are crystal palaces;
    From those skiey towers
    Where Thought's crowned powers
Sit watching your dance, ye happy Hours!

    From the dim recesses
    Of woven caresses,
Where lovers catch ye by your loose tresses;
    From the azure isles,
    Where sweet Wisdom smiles,
Delaying your ships with her siren wiles.   110

    From the temples high
    Of Man's ear and eye,
Roofed over Sculpture and Poesy;
    From the murmurings
    Of the unsealed springs
Where Science bedews her Dædal wings.

Years after years,
Through blood, and tears,
And a thick hell of hatreds, and hopes, and fears;
We waded and flew,   120
And the islets were few
Where the bud-blighted flowers of happiness grew.

Our feet now, every palm,
Are sandalled with calm,
And the dew of our wings is a rain of balm;
And, beyond our eyes,
The human love lies
Which makes all it gazes on Paradise.

CHORUS OF SPIRITS AND HOURS
Then weave the web of the mystic measure;
From the depths of the sky and the ends of the earth,
Come, swift Spirits of might and of pleasure, 131
Fill the dance and the music of mirth,
As the waves of a thousand streams rush by
To an ocean of splendour and harmony!

CHORUS OF SPIRITS
Our spoil is won,
Our task is done,
We are free to dive, or soar, or run;
Beyond and around,
Or within the bound
Which clips the world with darkness round. 140

We'll pass the eyes
Of the starry skies
Into the hoar deep to colonize:
Death, Chaos, and Night,

From the sound of our flight,
Shall flee, like mist from a tempest's might.

And Earth, Air, and Light,
And the Spirit of Might,
Which drives round the stars in their fiery flight;
And Love, Thought, and Breath, 150
The powers that quell Death,
Wherever we soar shall assemble beneath.

And our singing shall build
In the void's loose field
A world for the Spirit of Wisdom to wield;
We will take our plan
From the new world of man,
And our work shall be called the Promethean.

CHORUS OF HOURS

Break the dance, and scatter the song;
Let some depart, and some remain. 160

SEMICHORUS I

We, beyond heaven, are driven along:

SEMICHORUS II

Us the enchantments of earth retain:

SEMICHORUS I

Ceaseless, and rapid, and fierce, and free,
With the Spirits which build a new earth and sea,
And a heaven where yet heaven could never be,

SEMICHORUS II

Solemn, and slow, and serene, and bright,

Leading the Day and outspeeding the Night,
With the powers of a world of perfect light.

SEMICHORUS I
We whirl, singing loud, round the gathering sphere,
Till the trees, and the beasts, and the clouds appear   170
From its chaos made calm by love, not fear.

SEMICHORUS II
We encircle the ocean and mountains of earth,
And the happy forms of its death and birth
Change to the music of our sweet mirth.

CHORUS OF HOURS AND SPIRITS
Break the dance, and scatter the song,
   Let some depart, and some remain,
Wherever we fly we lead along
In leashes, like starbeams, soft yet strong,
   The clouds that are heavy with love's sweet rain.

PANTHEA Ha! they are gone!
IONE   Yet feel you no delight   180
From the past sweetness?
   PANTHEA   As the bare green hill
When some soft cloud vanishes into rain,
Laughs with a thousand drops of sunny water
To the unpavilioned sky!
   IONE   Even whilst we speak
New notes arise. What is that awful sound?
   PANTHEA 'Tis the deep music of the rolling world
Kindling within the strings of the waved air
Æolian modulations.
   IONE   Listen too,
How every pause is filled with under-notes,
Clear, silver, icy, keen, awakening tones,   190

86

Which pierce the sense, and live within the soul,
As the sharp stars pierce winter's crystal air
And gaze upon themselves within the sea.
    PANTHEA But see where through two openings in the forest
Which hanging branches overcanopy,
And where two runnels of a rivulet,
Between the close moss violet-inwoven,
Have made their path of melody, like sisters
Who part with sighs that they may meet in smiles,
Turning their dear disunion to an isle   200
Of lovely grief, a wood of sweet sad thoughts;
Two visions of strange radiance float upon
The ocean-like enchantment of strong sound,
Which flows intenser, keener, deeper yet
Under the ground and through the windless air.
    IONE I see a chariot like that thinnest boat,
In which the Mother of the Months is borne
By ebbing light into her western cave,
When she upsprings from interlunar dreams;
O'er which is curved an orblike canopy   210
Of gentle darkness, and the hills and woods,
Distinctly seen through that dusk aery veil,
Regard like shapes in an enchanter's glass;
Its wheels are solid clouds, azure and gold,
Such as the genii of the thunderstorm
Pile on the floor of the illumined sea
When the sun rushes under it; they roll
And move and grow as with an inward wind;
Within it sits a wingèd infant, white
Its countenance, like the whiteness of bright snow,   220
Its plumes are as feathers of sunny frost,
Its limbs gleam white, through the wind-flowing folds
Of its white robe, woof of ethereal pearl.
Its hair is white, the brightness of white light

Scattered in strings; yet its two eyes are heavens
Of liquid darkness, which the Deity
Within seems pouring, as a storm is poured
From jaggèd clouds, out of their arrowy lashes,
Tempering the cold and radiant air around,
With fire that is not brightness; in its hand   235
It sways a quivering moonbeam, from whose point
A guiding power directs the chariot's prow
Over its wheelèd clouds, which as they roll
Over the grass, and flowers, and waves, wake sounds,
Sweet as a singing rain of silver dew.

   PANTHEA And from the other opening in the wood
Rushes, with loud and whirlwind harmony,
A sphere, which is as many thousand spheres,
Solid as crystal, yet through all its mass
Flow, as through empty space, music and light: 241
Ten thousand orbs involving and involved,
Purple and azure, white, and green, and golden,
Sphere within sphere; and every space between
Peopled with unimaginable shapes,
Such as ghosts dream dwell in the lampless deep,
Yet each inter-transpicuous, and they whirl
Over each other with a thousand motions,
Upon a thousand sightless axles spinning,
And with the force of self-destroying swiftness,
Intensely, slowly, solemnly roll on,   250
Kindling with mingled sounds, and many tones,
Intelligible words and music wild.
With mighty whirl the multitudinous orb
Grinds the bright brook into an azure mist
Of elemental subtlety, like light;
And the wild odour of the forest flowers,
The music of the living grass and air,
The emerald light of leaf-entangled beams

Round its intense yet self-conflicting speed,
Seem kneaded into one aëreal mass   260
Which drowns the sense. Within the orb itself,
Pillowed upon its alabaster arms,
Like to a child o'erwearied with sweet toil,
On its own folded wings, and wavy hair,
The Spirit of the Earth is laid asleep,
And you can see its little lips are moving,
Amid the changing light of their own smiles,
Like one who talks of what he loves in dream.
    IONE 'Tis only mocking the orb's harmony.
    PANTHEA And from a star upon its forehead, shoot,   270
Like swords of azure fire, or golden spears
With tyrant-quelling myrtle overtwined,
Embleming heaven and earth united now,
Vast beams like spokes of some invisible wheel
Which whirl as the orb whirls, swifter than thought,
Filling the abyss with sun-like lightenings,
And perpendicular now, and now transverse,
Pierce the dark soil, and as they pierce and pass,
Make bare the secrets of the earth's deep heart;
Infinite mines of adamant and gold,   280
Valueless stones, and unimagined gems,
And caverns on crystalline columns poised
With vegetable silver overspread;
Wells of unfathomed fire, and water springs
Whence the great sea, even as a child is fed,
Whose vapours clothe earth's monarch mountain-tops
With kingly, ermine snow. The beams flash on
And make appear the melancholy ruins
Of cancelled cycles; anchors, beaks of ships;
Planks turned to marble; quivers, helms, and spears,   290
And gorgon-headed targes, and the wheels
Of scythèd chariots, and the emblazonry

Of trophies, standards, and armorial beasts,
Round which death laughed, sepulchred emblems
Of dead destruction, ruin within ruin!
The wrecks beside of many a city vast,
Whose population which the earth grew over
Was mortal, but not human; see, they lie,
Their monstrous works, and uncouth skeletons,
Their statues, homes and fanes; prodigious shapes   300
Huddled in gray annihilation, split,
Jammed in the hard, black deep; and over these,
The anatomies of unknown wingèd things,
And fishes which were isles of living scale,
And serpents, bony chains, twisted around
The iron crags, or within heaps of dust
To which the tortuous strength of their last pangs
Had crushed the iron crags; and over these
The jaggèd alligator, and the might
Of earth-convulsing behemoth, which once   310
Were monarch beasts, and on the slimy shores,
And weed-overgrown continents of earth,
Increased and multiplied like summer worms
On an abandoned corpse, till the blue globe
Wrapped deluge round it like a cloak, and they
Yelled, gasped, and were abolished; or some God
Whose throne was in a comet, passed, and cried,
'Be not!' And like my words they were no more.

THE EARTH

The joy, the triumph, the delight, the madness!
The boundless, overflowing, bursting gladness,   320
The vaporous exultation not to be confined!
Ha! ha! the animation of delight
Which wraps me, like an atmosphere of light,
And bears me as a cloud is borne by its own wind.

THE MOON

Brother mine, calm wanderer,
Happy globe of land and air,
Some Spirit is darted like a beam from thee,
Which penetrates my frozen frame,
And passes with the warmth of flame,
With love, and odour, and deep melody   330
Through me, through me!

THE EARTH

Ha! ha! the caverns of my hollow mountains,
My cloven fire-crags, sound-exulting fountains,
Laugh with a vast and inextinguishable laughter.
The oceans, and the deserts, and the abysses.
And the deep air's unmeasured wildernesses,
Answer from all their clouds and billows, echoing after.

They cry aloud as I do. Sceptred curse,
Who all our green and azure universe
Threatenedst to muffle round with black destruction, sending 340
A solid cloud to rain hot thunderstones,
And splinter and knead down my children's bones,
All I bring forth, to one void mass battering and blending,—

Until each crag-like tower, and storied column.
Palace, and obelisk, and temple solemn,
My imperial mountains crowned with cloud, and snow, and fire;
My sea-like forests, every blade and blossom
Which finds a grave or cradle in my bosom,
Were stamped by thy strong hate into a lifeless mire:

How art thou sunk, withdrawn, covered, drunk up   350
By thirsty nothing, as the brackish cup
Drained by a desert-troop, a little drop for all;

And from beneath, around, within, above,
Filling thy void annihilation, love
Burst in like light on caves cloven by the thunder-ball.

THE MOON

The snow upon my lifeless mountains
Is loosened into living fountains,
My solid oceans flow, and sing, and shine:
A spirit from my heart bursts forth,
It clothes with unexpected birth 360
My cold bare bosom: Oh! it must be thine
On mine, on mine!

Gazing on thee I feel I know,
Green stalks burst forth, and bright flowers grow,
And living shapes upon my bosom move:
Music is in the sea and air,
Wingèd clouds soar here and there,
Dark with the rain new buds are dreaming of:
'Tis love, all love!

THE EARTH

It interpenetrates my granite mass, 370
Through tangled roots and trodden clay doth pass
Into the utmost leaves and delicatest flowers;
Upon the winds, among the clouds 'tis spread,
It wakes a life in the forgotten dead,
They breathe a spirit up from their obscurest bowers.

And like a storm bursting its cloudy prison
With thunder, and with whirlwind, has arisen
Out of the lampless caves of unimagined being:
With earthquake shock and swiftness making shiver
Thought's stagnant chaos, unremoved for ever, 380
Till hate, and fear, and pain, light-vanquished shadows, fleeing,

Leave Man, who was a many-sided mirror,
　Which could distort to many a shape of error,
This true fair world of things, a sea reflecting love;
　Which over all his kind, as the sun's heaven
　Gliding o'er ocean, smooth, serene, and even,
Darting from starry depths radiance and life, doth move:

Leave Man, even as a leprous child is left,
　Who follows a sick beast to some warm cleft
Of rocks, through which the might of healing springs is poured;
　Then when it wanders home with rosy smile,　　　　391
　Unconscious, and its mother fears awhile
It is a spirit, then, weeps on her child restored.

Man, oh, not men! a chain of linkèd thought,
　Of love and might to be divided not,
Compelling the elements with adamantine stress;
　As the sun rules, even with a tyrant's gaze,
　The unquiet republic of the maze
Of planets, struggling fierce towards heaven's free wilderness.

Man, one harmonious soul of many a soul,　　　　400
　Whose nature is its own divine control,
Where all things flow to all, as rivers to the sea;
　Familiar acts are beautiful through love;
　Labour, and pain, and grief, in life's green grove
Sport like tame beasts, none knew how gentle they could be!

His will, with all mean passions, bad delights,
　And selfish cares, its trembling satellites,
A spirit ill to guide, but mighty to obey,
　Is as a tempest-wingèd ship, whose helm
　Love rules, through waves which dare not overwhelm,　410
Forcing life's wildest shores to own its sovereign sway.

All things confess his strength. Through the cold mass
Of marble and of colour his dreams pass;
Bright threads whence mothers weave the robes their children
    wear;
  Language is a perpetual Orphic song,
  Which rules with Dædal harmony a throng
Of thoughts and forms, which else senseless and shapeless were.

  The lightning is his slave; heaven's utmost deep
  Gives up her stars, and like a flock of sheep
They pass before his eye, are numbered, and roll on!   420
  The tempest is his steed, he strides the air;
  And the abyss shouts from her depth laid bare,
Heaven, hast thou secrets? Man unveils me; I have none.

THE MOON
The shadow of white death has passed
From my path in heaven at last,
  A clinging shroud of solid frost and sleep;
    And through my newly-woven bowers,
    Wander happy paramours,
  Less mighty, but as mild as those who keep
      Thy vales more deep.   430

THE EARTH
As the dissolving warmth of dawn may fold
A half unfrozen dew-globe, green, and gold,
And crystalline, till it becomes a wingèd mist,
  And wanders up the vault of the blue day,
  Outlives the moon, and on the sun's last ray
Hangs o'er the sea, a fleece of fire and amethyst.

THE MOON
Thou art folded, thou art lying
In the light which is undying

Of thine own joy, and heaven's smile divine;
  All suns and constellations shower   440
    On thee a light, a life, a power
Which doth array thy sphere; thou pourest thine
      On mine, on mine!

THE EARTH

I spin beneath my pyramid of night,
  Which points into the heavens dreaming delight,
Murmuring victorious joy in my enchanted sleep;
  As a youth lulled in love-dreams faintly sighing,
    Under the shadow of his beauty lying,
Which round his rest a watch of light and warmth doth keep.

THE MOON

As in the soft and sweet eclipse,   450
  When soul meets soul on lovers' lips,
High hearts are calm, and brightest eyes are dull;
  So when thy shadow falls on me,
    Then am I mute and still, by thee
Covered; of thy love, Orb most beautiful,
      Full, oh, too full!

Thou art speeding round the sun
  Brightest world of many a one;
Green and azure sphere which shinest
  With a light which is divinest   460
Among all the lamps of Heaven
  To whom life and light is given;
I, thy crystal paramour
  Borne beside thee by a power
Like the polar Paradise,
  Magnet-like of lovers' eyes;
I, a most enamoured maiden

95

Whose weak brain is overladen
With the pleasure of her love,
Maniac-like around thee move   470
Gazing, an insatiate bride,
On thy form from every side
Like a Mænad, round the cup
Which Agave lifted up
In the weird Cadmæan forest.
Brother, wheresoe'er thou soarest
I must hurry, whirl and follow
Through the heavens wide and hollow,
Sheltered by the warm embrace
Of thy soul from hungry space,   480
Drinking from thy sense and sight
Beauty, majesty, and might,
As a lover or a chameleon
Grows like what it looks upon,
As a violet's gentle eye
Gazes on the azure sky
Until its hue grows like what it beholds,
As a gray and watery mist
Glows like solid amethyst
Athwart the western mountain it enfolds,   490
When the sunset sleeps
Upon its snow—

THE EARTH

And the weak day weeps
That it should be so.
Oh, gentle Moon, the voice of thy delight
Falls on me like thy clear and tender light
Soothing the seaman, borne the summer night,
Through isles forever calm;
Oh, gentle Moon, thy crystal accents pierce

The caverns of my pride's deep universe,
Charming the tiger joy, whose tramplings fierce
  Made wounds which need thy balm.
    PANTHEA   I rise as from a bath of sparkling water,
A bath of azure light, among dark rocks,
Out of the stream of sound.
    IONE   Ah me! sweet sister,
The stream of sound has ebbed away from us,
And you pretend to rise out of its wave,
Because your words fall like the clear, soft dew
Shaken from a bathing wood-nymph's limbs and hair.
    PANTHEA   Peace! peace! A mighty Power, which is as
        darkness,   510
Is rising out of Earth, and from the sky
Is showered like night, and from within the air
Bursts, like eclipse which had been gathered up
Into the pores of sunlight: the bright visions,
Wherein the singing spirits rode and shone,
Gleam like pale meteors through a watery night.
    IONE   There is a sense of words upon mine ear.
    PANTHEA   An universal sound like words: Oh, list!

                    DEMOGORGON
    Thou, Earth, calm empire of a happy soul,
      Sphere of divinest shapes and harmonies,   520
    Beautiful orb! gathering as thou dost roll
      The love which paves thy path along the skies:

                    THE EARTH
    I hear: I am as a drop of dew that dies.

                    DEMOGORGON
    Thou, Moon, which gazest on the nightly Earth
      With wonder, as it gazes upon thee;
                        97

Whilst each to men, and beasts, and the swift birth
Of birds, is beauty, love, calm, harmony:

THE MOON
I hear: I am a leaf shaken by thee!

DEMOGORGON
Ye Kings of suns and stars, Dæmons and Gods,
  Aetherial Dominations, who possess   530
Elysian, windless, fortunate abodes
  Beyond Heaven's constellated wilderness:

A VOICE FROM ABOVE
Our great Republic hears, we are blest, and bless.

DEMOGORGON
Ye happy Dead, whom beams of brightest verse
  Are clouds to hide, not colours to portray,
Whether your nature is that universe
  Which once ye saw and suffered—

A VOICE FROM BENEATH
                         Or as they
Whom we have left, we change and pass away.

DEMOGORGON
Ye elemental Genii, who have homes
  From man's high mind even to the central stone   540
Of sullen lead; from heaven's star-fretted domes
  To the dull weed some sea-worm battens on:

A CONFUSED VOICE
We hear: thy words waken Oblivion.

Spirits, whose homes are flesh: ye beasts and birds,
  Ye worms, and fish; ye living leaves and buds;
Lightning and wind; and ye untameable herds,
  Meteors and mists, which throng air's solitudes:--

Thy voice to us is wind among still woods.

Man, who wert once a despot and a slave;
  A dupe and a deceiver; a decay;   550
A traveller from the cradle to the grave
  Through the dim night of this immortal day:

Speak: thy strong words may never pass away.

This is the day, which down the void abysm
At the Earth-born's spell yawns for Heaven's despotism,
  And Conquest is dragged captive through the deep:
Love, from its awful throne of patient power
In the wise heart, from the last giddy hour
  Of dread endurance, from the slippery, steep,
And narrow verge of crag-like agony, springs   560
And folds over the world its healing wings.

Gentleness, Virtue, Wisdom, and Endurance,
These are the seals of that most firm assurance
  Which bars the pit over Destruction's strength;
And if, with infirm hand, Eternity,
Mother of many acts and hours, should free
  The serpent that would clasp her with his length;

These are the spells by which to reassume
An empire o'er the disentangled doom.

To suffer woes which Hope thinks infinite;   570
To forgive wrongs darker than death or night;
  To defy Power, which seems omnipotent;
To love, and bear; to hope till Hope creates
From its own wreck the thing it contemplates;
  Neither to change, not falter, nor repent;
This, like thy glory, Titan, is to be
Good, great and joyous, beautiful and free;
This is alone Life, Joy, Empire, and Victory.

The Triumph of Life

Swift as a spirit hastening to his task
Of glory and of good, the Sun sprang forth
Rejoicing in his splendour, and the mask
Of darkness fell from the awakened Earth—
The smokeless altars of the mountain snows
Flamed above crimson clouds, and at the birth
Of light, the Ocean's orison arose,
To which the birds tempered their matin lay.
All flowers in field or forest which unclose
Their trembling eyelids to the kiss of day,   10
Swinging their censers in the element,
With orient incense lit by the new ray
Burned slow and inconsumably, and sent
Their odorous sighs up to the smiling air;
And, in succession due, did continent,
Isle, ocean, and all things that in them wear

The form and character of mortal mould,
Rise as the Sun their fathers rose, to bear
Their portion of the toil, which he of old
Took as his own, and then imposed on them: 20
But I, whom thoughts which must remain untold
Had kept as wakeful as the stars that gem
The cone of night, now they were laid asleep
Stretched my faint limbs beneath the hoary stem
Which an old chestnut flung athwart the steep
Of a green Apennine: before me fled
The night; behind me rose the day; the deep
Was at my feet, and Heaven above my head,—
When a strange trance over my fancy grew
Which was not slumber, for the shade it spread   30
Was so transparent, that the scene came through
As clear as when a veil of light is drawn
O'er evening hills they glimmer; and I knew
That I had felt the freshness of that dawn
Bathe in the same cold dew my brow and hair,
And sate as thus upon that slope of lawn
Under the self-same bough, and heard as there
The birds, the fountains and the ocean hold
Sweet talk in music through the enamoured air,
And then a vision on my brain was rolled.   40

As in that trance of wondrous thought I lay,
This was the tenour of my waking dream:—
Methought I sate beside a public way
Thick strewn with summer dust, and a great stream
Of people there was hurrying to and fro,
Numerous as gnats upon the evening gleam,
All hastening onward, yet none seemed to know
Whither he went, or whence he came, or why
He made one of the multitude, and so

Was borne amid the crowd, as through the sky   50
One of the million leaves of summer's bier;
Old age and youth, manhood and infancy,
Mixed in one mighty torrent did appear,
Some flying from the thing they feared, and some
Seeking the object of another's fear;
And others, as with steps towards the tomb,
Pored on the trodden worms that crawled beneath,
And others mournfully within the gloom
Of their own shadow walked, and called it death;
And some fled from it as it were a ghost,   60
Half fainting in the affliction of vain breath:
But more, with motions which each other crossed,
Pursued or shunned the shadows the clouds threw,
Or birds within the noonday aether lost,
Upon that path where flowers never grew,—
And, weary with vain toil and faint for thirst,
Heard not the fountains, whose melodious dew
Out of their mossy cells forever burst;
Nor felt the breeze which from the forest told
Of grassy paths and wood-lawns interspersed   70
With overarching elms and caverns cold,
And violet banks where sweet dreams brood, but they
Pursued their serious folly as of old.

And as I gazed, methought that in the way
The throng grew wilder, as the woods of June
When the south wind shakes the extinguished day,
And a cold glare, intenser than the noon,
But icy cold, obscured with blinding light
The sun, as he the stars. Like the young moon—
When on the sunlit limits of the night   80
Her white shell trembles amid crimson air,
And whilst the sleeping tempest gathers might—

Doth, as the herald of its coming, bear
The ghost of its dead mother, whose dim form
Bends in dark aether from her infant's chair,—
So came a chariot on the silent storm
Of its own rushing splendour, and a Shape
So sate within, as one whom years deform,
Beneath a dusky hood and double cape,
Crouching within the shadow of a tomb;   90
And o'er what seemed the head a cloud-like crape
Was bent, a dun and faint aethereal gloom
Tempering the light. Upon the chariot-beam
A Janus-visaged Shadow did assume
The guidance of that wonder-wingèd team;
The shapes which drew it in thick lightenings
Were lost:—I heard alone on the air's soft stream
The music of their ever-moving wings.
All the four faces of that Charioteer
Had their eyes banded; little profit brings   100
Speed in the van and blindness in the rear,
Nor then avail the beams that quench the sun,—
Or that with banded eyes could pierce the sphere
Of all that is, has been or will be done;
So ill was the car guided—but it passed
With solemn speed majestically on.

The crowd gave way, and I arose aghast,
Or seemed to rise, so mighty was the trance,
And saw, like clouds upon the thunder-blast,
The million with fierce song and maniac dance   110
Raging around—such seemed the jubilee
As when to greet some conqueror's advance
Imperial Rome poured forth her living sea
From senate-house, and forum, and theatre,
When   upon the free

Had bound a yoke, which soon they stooped to bear.
Nor wanted here the just similitude
Of a triumphal pageant, for where'er
The chariot rolled, a captive multitude
Was driven;—all those who had grown old in power   120
Or misery,—all who had their age subdued
By action or by suffering, and whose hour
Was drained to its last sand in weal or woe,
So that the trunk survived both fruit and flower;—
All those whose fame or infamy must grow
Till the great winter lay the form and name
Of this green earth with them for ever low;—
All but the sacred few who could not tame
Their spirits to the conquerors—but as soon
As they had touched the world with living flame,   130
Fled back like eagles to their native noon,
Or those who put aside the diadem
Of earthly thrones or gems . . .
Were there, of Athens or Jerusalem,
Were neither mid the mighty captives seen,
Nor mid the ribald crowd that followed them,
Nor those who went before fierce and obscene.
The wild dance maddens in the van, and those
Who lead it—fleet as shadows on the green,
Outspeed the chariot, and without repose   140
Mix with each other in tempestuous measure
To savage music, wilder as it grows,
They, tortured by their agonizing pleasure,
Convulsed and on the rapid whirlwinds spun
Of that fierce Spirit, whose unholy leisure
Was soothed by mischief since the world begun,
Throw back their heads and loose their streaming hair;
And in their dance round her who dims the sun,
Maidens and youths fling their wild arms in air

As their feet twinkle; they recede, and now   150
Bending within each others atmosphere,
Kindle invisibly—and as they glow,
Like moths by light attracted and repelled,
Oft to their bright destruction come and go,
Till like two clouds into one vale impelled,
That shake the mountains when their lightnings mingle
And die in rain—the fiery band which held
Their natures, snaps—while the shock still may tingle,
One falls and then another in the path
Senseless—nor is the desolation single,   160
Yet ere I can say *where*—the chariot hath
Passed over them—not other trace I find
But as of foam after the ocean's wrath
Is spent upon the desert shore;—behind,
Old men and women foully disarrayed,
Shake their gray hairs in the insulting wind,
And follow in the dance, with limbs decayed,
Seeking to reach the light which leaves them still
Farther behind and deeper in the shade.
But not the less with impotence of will   170
They wheel, though ghastly shadows interpose
Round them and round each other, and fulfil
Their work, and in the dust from whence they rose
Sink, and corruption veils them as they lie,
And past in these performs what   in those.

Struck to the heart by this sad pageantry,
Half to myself I said—'And what is this?
Whose shape is that within the car? And why—'
I would have added—'is all here amiss?—'
But a voice answered—'Life!'—I turned, and knew   180
(O Heaven, have mercy on such wretchedness!)
That what I thought was an old root which grew

To strange distortion out of the hill side,
Was indeed one of those deluded crew,
And that the grass, which methought hung so wide
And white, was but his thin discoloured hair,
And that the holes he vainly sought to hide,
Were or had been eyes:—'If thou canst, forbear
To join the dance, which I had well forborne!'
Said the grim Feature (of my thought aware).   190
'I will unfold that which to this deep scorn
Led me and my companions, and relate
The progress of the pageant since the morn;
If thirst of knowledge shall not then abate,
Follow it thou even to the night, but I
Am weary.'—Then like one who with the weight
Of his own words is staggered, wearily
He paused; and ere he could resume, I cried:
'First, who art thou?'—'Before thy memory,
I feared, loved, hated, suffered, did and died,   200
And if the spark with which Heaven lit my spirit
Had been with purer nutriment supplied,
Corruption would not now thus much inherit
Of what was once Rousseau,—nor this disguise
Stain that which ought to have disdained to wear it;
If I have been extinguished, yet there rise
A thousand beacons from the spark I bore'—
'And who are those chained to the car?'—'The wise,
The great, the unforgotten,—they who wore
Mitres and helms and crowns, or wreaths of light,   210
Signs of thought's empire over thought—their lore
Taught them not this, to know themselves; their might
Could not repress the mystery within
And for the morn of truth they feigned, deep night
Caught them ere evening.'—'Who is he with chin
Upon his breast, and hands crossed on his chain?'—

The child of a fierce hour; he sought to win
The world, and lost all that it did contain
Of greatness, in its hope destroyed; and more
Of fame and peace than virtue's self can gain   220
Without the opportunity which bore
Him on its eagle pinions to the peak
From which a thousand climbers have before
Fallen, as Napoleon fell.'—I felt my cheek
Alter, to see the shadow pass away,
Whose grasp had left the giant world so weak
That every pigmy kicked it as it lay;
And much I grieved to think how power and will
In opposition rule our mortal day,
And why God made irreconcilable   230
Good and the means of good; and for despair
I half disdained mine eyes' desire to fill
With the spent vision of the times that were
And scarce have ceased to be.—'Dost thou behold,'
Said my guide, 'those spoilers spoiled, Voltaire,
Frederick, and Paul, Catherine, and Leopold,
And hoary anarchs, demagogues, and sage—
      names which the world thinks always old,
For in the battle Life and they did wage,
She remained conqueror. I was overcome   240
By my own heart alone, which neither age,
Nor tears, nor infamy, nor now the tomb
Could temper to its object.'

                              'Let them pass,'
I cried, 'the world and its mysterious doom
Is not so much more glorious than it was,
That I desire to worship those who drew
New figures on its false and fragile glass
As the old faded.'—'Figures ever new

Rise on the bubble, paint them as you may;
We have but thrown, as those before us threw,   250
Our shadows on it as it passed away.
But mark how chained to the triumphal chair
The mighty phantoms of an elder day;
All that is mortal of great Plato there
Expiates the joy and woe his master knew not;
The star that ruled his doom was far too fair,
And life, where long that flower of Heaven grew not,
Conquered that heart by love, which gold, or pain,
Or age, or sloth, or slavery could subdue not.
And near him walk the   twain,   260
The tutor and his pupil, whom Dominion
Followed as tame as vulture in a chain.
The world was darkened beneath either pinion
Of him from whom the flock of conquerors
Fame singled out for her thunder-bearing minion;
The other long outlived both woes and wars,
Throned in the thoughts of men, and still had kept
The jealous key of Truth's eternal doors,
If Bacon's eagle spirit had not lept
Like lightning out of darkness—he compelled   270
The Proteus shape of Nature, as it slept
To wake, and lead him to the caves that held
The treasure of the secrets of its reign.
See the great bards of elder time, who quelled
The passions which they sung, as by their strain
May well be known: their living melody
Tempers its own contagion to the vein
Of those who are infected with it—I
Have suffered what I wrote, or viler pain!
And so my words have seeds of misery—   280
Even as the deeds of others, not as theirs.'
And then he pointed to a company,

'Midst whom I quickly recognized the heirs
Of Caesar's crime, from him to Constantine;
The anarch chiefs, whose force and murderous snares
Had founded many a sceptre-bearing line,
And spread the plague of gold and blood abroad:
And Gregory and John, and men divine,
Who rose like shadows between man and God;
Till that eclipse, still hanging over heaven,   290
Was worshipped by the world o'er which they strode,
For the true sun it quenched—'Their power was given
But to destroy,' replied the leader:—'I
Am one of those who have created, even
If it be but a world of agony.'—
'Whence camest thou? and whither goest thou?
How did thy course begin?' I said, 'and why?
Mine eyes are sick of this perpetual flow
Of people, and my heart sick of one sad thought—
Speak!'—'Whence I am, I partly seem to know,   300
And how and by what paths I have been brought
To this dread pass, methinks even thou mayst guess;—
Why this should be, my mind can compass not;
Whither the conqueror hurries me, still less;—
But follow thou, and from spectator turn
Actor or victim in this wretchedness,
And what thou wouldst be taught I then may learn
From thee. Now listen:—

                    In the April prime,
When all the forest-tips began to burn
With kindling green, touched by the azure clime   310
Of the young season, I was laid asleep
Under a mountain, which from unknown time
Had yawned into a cavern, high and deep;
And from it came a gentle rivulet,

Whose water, like clear air, in its calm sweep
Bent the soft grass, and kept for ever wet
The stems of the sweet flowers, and filled the grove
With sounds, which whoso hears must needs forget
All pleasure and all pain, all hate and love,
Which they had known before that hour of rest;   320
A sleeping mother then would dream not of
Her only child who died upon the breast
At eventide—a king would mourn no more
The crown of which his brows were dispossessed
When the sun lingered o'er his ocean floor
To gild his rival's new prosperity.
Thou wouldst forget thus vainly to deplore
Ills, which if ills can find no cure from thee,
The thought of which no other sleep will quell,
Nor other music blot from memory,   330
So sweet and deep is the oblivious spell;
And whether life had been before that sleep
The Heaven which I imagine, or a Hell
Like this harsh world in which I wake to weep,
I know not.

             I arose, and for a space
The scene of woods and waters seemed to keep,
Though it was now broad day, a gentle trace
Of light diviner than the common sun
Sheds on the common earth, and all the place
Was filled with magic sounds woven into one   340
Oblivious melody, confusing sense
Amid the gliding waves and shadows dun;
And, as I looked, the bright omnipresence
Of morning through the orient cavern flowed,
And the sun's image radiantly intense
Burned on the waters of the well that glowed

Like gold, and threaded all the forest's maze
With winding paths of emerald fire; there stood
Amid the sun, as he amid the blaze
Of his own glory, on the vibrating 350
Floor of the fountain, paved with flashing rays,
A Shape all light, which with one hand did fling
Dew on the earth, as if she were the dawn,
And the invisible rain did ever sing
A silver music on the mossy lawn;
And still before me on the dusky grass,
Iris her many-coloured scarf had drawn:
In her right hand she bore a crystal glass,
Mantling with bright Nepenthe; the fierce splendour
Fell from her as she moved under the mass 360
Of the deep cavern, and with palms so tender,
Their tread broke not the mirror of its billow,
Glided along the river, and did bend her
Head under the dark boughs, till like a willow
Her fair hair swept the bosom of the stream
That whispered with delight to be its pillow.
As one enamoured is upborne in dream
O'er lily-paven lakes, mid silver mist,
To wondrous music, so this shape might seem
Partly to tread the waves with feet which kissed 370
The dancing foam; partly to glide along
The air which roughened the moist amethyst,
Or the faint morning beams that fell among
The trees, or the soft shadows of the trees;
And her feet, ever to the ceaseless song
Of leaves, and winds, and waves, and birds, and bees,
And falling drops, moved in a measure new
Yet sweet, as on the summer evening breeze,
Up from the lake a shape of golden dew
Between two rocks, athwart the rising moon, 380

III

Dances i' the wind, where never eagle flew;
And still her feet, no less than the sweet tune
To which they moved, seemed as they moved to blot
The thoughts of him who gazed on them; and soon
All that was, seemed as if it had been not;
And all the gazer's mind was strewn beneath
Her feet like embers; and she, thought by thought,
Trampled its sparks into the dust of death;
As day upon the threshold of the east
Treads out the lamps of night, until the breath   390
Of darkness re-illumine even the least
Of heaven's living eyes—like day she came,
Making the night a dream; and ere she ceased
To move, as one between desire and shame
Suspended, I said—'If, as it doth seem,
Thou comest from the realm without a name
Into this valley of perpetual dream,
Show whence I came, and where I am, and why—
Pass not away upon the passing stream.'
'Arise and quench thy thirst,' was her reply.   400
And as a shut lily stricken by the wand
Of dewy morning's vital alchemy,
I rose; and, bending at her sweet command,
Touched with faint lips the cup she raised,
And suddenly my brain became as sand
Where the first wave had more than half erased
The track of deer on desert Labrador;
Whilst the wolf, from which they fled amazed,
Leaves his stamp visibly upon the shore,
Until the second bursts;—   410

                                             So on my sight
Burst a new vision, never seen before,
And the fair shape waned in the coming light,

112

As veil by veil the silent splendour drops
From Lucifer, amid the chrysolite
Of sunrise, ere it tinge the mountain-tops;
And as the presence of that fairest planet,
Although unseen, is felt by one who hopes
That his day's path may end as he began it,
In that star's smile, whose light is like the scent
Of a jonquil when evening breezes fan it,   420
Or the soft note in which his dear lament
The Brescian[1] shepherd breathes, or the caress
That turned his weary slumber to content;
So knew I in that light's severe excess
The presence of that Shape which on the stream
Moved, as I moved along the wilderness,
More dimly than a day-appearing dream,
The ghost of a forgotten form of sleep;
A light of heaven, whose half-extinguished beam
Through the sick day in which we wake to weep   430
Glimmers, for ever sought, for ever lost;
So did that shape its obscure tenour keep
Beside my path, as silent as a ghost;
But the new Vision, and the cold bright car,
With solemn speed and stunning music, crossed
The forest, and as if from some dread war
Triumphantly returning, the loud million
Fiercely extolled the fortune of her star.
A moving arch of victory, the vermilion
And green and azure plumes of Iris had   440
Built high over her wind-wingèd pavilion,
And underneath aethereal glory clad
The wilderness, and far before her flew
The tempest of the splendour, which forbade

[1]The favourite song, *stanco di pascolor la pecorelle*, is a Brescian national air.—
[Mrs. Shelley's note.]

Shadow to fall from leaf and stone; the crew
Seemed in that light, like atomies to dance
Within a sunbeam;—some upon the new
Embroidery of flowers, that did enhance
The grassy vesture of the desert, played,
Forgetful of the chariot's swift advance;   450
Others stood gazing, till within the shade
Of the great mountain its light left them dim;
Others outspeeded it; and others made
Circles around it, like the clouds that swim
Round the high moon in a bright sea of air;
And more did follow, with exulting hymn,
The chariot and the captives fettered there:—
But all like bubbles on an eddying flood
Fell into the same track at last, and were
Borne onward.—I among the multitude   460
Was swept—me, sweetest flowers delayed not long;
Me, not the shadow nor the solitude;
Me, not that falling stream's Lethean song;
Me, not the phantom of that early Form
Which moved upon its motion—but among
The thickest billows of that living storm
I plunged, and bared my bosom to the clime
Of that cold light, whose airs too soon deform.

Before the chariot had begun to climb
The opposing steep of that mysterious dell,   470
Behold a wonder worthy of the rhyme
Of him who from the lowest depths of hell,
Through every paradise and through all glory,
Love led serene, and who returned to tell
The words of hate and awe; the wondrous story
How all things are transfigured except Love;
For deaf as is a sea, which wrath makes hoary,

The world can hear not the sweet notes that move
The sphere whose light is melody to lovers—
A wonder worthy of his rhyme.—The grove   480
Grew dense with shadows to its inmost covers,
The earth was gray with phantoms, and the air
Was peopled with dim forms, as when there hovers
A flock of vampire-bats before the glare
Of the tropic sun, bringing, ere evening,
Strange night upon some Indian isle;—thus were
Phantoms diffused around; and some did fling
Shadows of shadows, yet unlike themselves,
Behind them; some like eaglets on the wing
Were lost in the white day; others like elves   490
Danced in a thousand unimagined shapes
Upon the sunny streams and grassy shelves;
And others sate chattering like restless apes
On vulgar hands, . . .
Some made a cradle of the ermined capes
Of kingly mantles; some across the tiar
Of pontiffs sate like vultures; others played
Under the crown which girt with empire
A baby's or an idiot's brow, and made
Their nests in it. The old anatomies   500
Sate hatching their bare broods under the shade
Of daemon wings, and laughed from their dead eyes
To reassume the delegated power,
Arrayed in which those worms did monarchize,
Who made this earth their charnel. Others more
Humble, like falcons, sate upon the fist
Of common men, and round their heads did soar;
Or like small gnats and flies, as thick as mist
On evening marshes, thronged about the brow
Of lawyers, statesmen, priest and theorist;—   510
And others, like discoloured flakes of snow

On fairest bosoms and the sunniest hair,
Fell, and were melted by the youthful glow
Which they extinguished; and, like tears, they were
A veil to those from whose faint lids they rained
In drops of sorrow. I became aware
Of whence those forms proceeded which thus stained
The track in which we moved. After brief space,
From every form the beauty slowly waned;
From every firmest limb and fairest face   520
The strength and freshness fell like dust, and left
The action and the shape without the grace
Of life. The marble brow of youth was cleft
With care; and in those eyes where once hope shone,
Desire, like a lioness bereft
Of her last cub, glared ere it died; each one
Of that great crowd sent forth incessantly
These shadows, numerous as the dead leaves blown
In autumn evening from a poplar tree.
Each like himself and like each other were   530
At first; but some distorted seemed to be
Obscure clouds, moulded by the casual air;
And of this stuff the car's creative ray
Wrought all the busy phantoms that were there,
As the sun shapes the clouds; thus on the way
Mask after mask fell from the countenance
And form of all; and long before the day
Was old, the joy which waked like heaven's glance
The sleepers in the oblivious valley, died;
And some grew weary of the ghastly dance,   540
And fell, as I have fallen, by the wayside;—
Those soonest from whose forms most shadows passed,
And least of strength and beauty did abide.

Then what is life? I cried.'—

VERSE TRANSLATIONS BY SHELLEY

From

Homer's Hymn to Mercury

. . . Seized with a sudden fancy for fresh meat,
He in his sacred crib deposited
  The hollow lyre, and from the cavern sweet
Rushed with great leaps up to the mountain's head,
  Revolving in his mind some subtle feat
Of thievish craft, such as a swindler might
Devise in the lone season of dun night.

Lo! the great Sun under the ocean's bed has
  Driven steeds and chariot—the child meanwhile strode
O'er the Pierian mountains clothed in shadows,
  Where the immortal oxen of the God
Are pastured in the flowering unmown meadows,
  And safely stalled in a remote abode.—
The archer Argicide, elate and proud,
Drove fifty from the herd, lowing aloud.

He drove them wandering o'er the sandy way,
  But, being ever mindful of his craft,
Backward and forward drove he them astray,
  So that the tracks which seemed before, were aft;
His sandals then he threw to the ocean spray,
  And for each foot he wrought a kind of raft
Of tamarisk, and tamarisk-like sprigs,
And bound them in a lump with withy twigs.

And on his feet he tied these sandals light,
The trail of whose wide leaves might not betray
    His track; and then, a self-sufficing wight,
Like a man hastening on some distant way,
    He from Pieria's mountain bent his flight;
But an old man perceived the infant pass
Down green Onchestus heaped like beds with grass.

The old man stood dressing his sunny vine:
    'Halloo! old fellow with the crookèd shoulder!
You grub those stumps? before they will bear wine:
    Methinks even you must grow a little older:
Attend, I pray, to this advice of mine,
    As you would 'scape what might appal a bolder—
Seeing, see not—and hearing, hear not—and—
If you have understanding—understand.'

So saying, Hermes roused the oxen vast;
    O'er shadowy mountain and resounding dell,
And flower-paven plains, great Hermes passed;
    Till the black night divine, which favouring fell
Around his steps, grew gray, and morning fast
    Wakened the world to work, and from her cell
Sea-strewn, the Pallantean Moon sublime
Into her watch-tower just began to climb.

Now to Alpheus he had driven all
    The broad-foreheaded oxen of the Sun;
They came unwearied to the lofty stall
    And to the water-troughs which ever run
Through the fresh fields—and when with rushgrass tall,
    Lotus and all sweet herbage, every one
Had pastured been, the great God made them move
Towards the stall in a collected drove.

A mighty pile of wood the God then heaped,
    And having soon conceived the mystery
Of fire, from two smooth laurel branches stripped
    The bark, and rubbed them in his palms;—on high
Suddenly forth the burning vapour leaped
    And the divine child saw delightedly.—
Mercury first found out for human weal
Tinder-box, matches, fire-irons, flint and steel. . . .
    [*Mercury slaughters two of the cattle and apportions them among
the gods, then returns to his cradle.*]
                                    . . . meanwhile the day

Aethereal born arose out of the flood
    Of flowing Ocean, bearing light to men.
Apollo passed toward the sacred wood,
    Which from the inmost depths of its green glen
Echoes the voice of Neptune,—and there stood
    On the same spot in green Onchestus then
That same old animal, the vine-dresser,
Who was employed hedging his vineyard there.

Latona's glorious Son began:—'I pray
    Tell, ancient hedger of Onchestus green,
Whether a drove of kine has passed this way,
    All heifers with crooked horns? for they have been
Stolen from the herd in high Pieria,
    Where a black bull was fed apart, between
Two woody mountains in a neighbouring glen,
And four fierce dogs watched there, unanimous as men.

'And what is strange, the author of this theft
    Has stolen the fatted heifers every one,
But the four dogs and the black bull are left:—
    Stolen they were last night at set of sun,

Of their soft beds and their sweet food bereft.—
   Now tell me, man born ere the world begun,
Have you seen anyone pass with the cows?'—
To whom the man of overhanging brows:

'My friend, it would require no common skill
   Justly to speak of everything I see:
On various purposes of good or ill
   Many pass by my vineyard,—and to me
'Tis difficult to know the invisible
   Thoughts, which in all those many minds may be:—
Thus much alone I certainly can say,
I tilled these vines till the decline of day,

'And then I thought I saw, but dare not speak
   With certainty of such a wondrous thing,
A child, who could not have been born a week,
   Those fair-horned cattle closely following,
And in his hand he held a polished stick:
   And, as on purpose, he walked wavering
From one side to the other of the road,
And with his face opposed the steps he trod.'

Apollo hearing this, passed quickly on—
   No wingèd omen could have shown more clear
That the deceiver was his father's son.
   So the God wraps a purple atmosphere
Around his shoulders, and like fire is gone
   To famous Pylos, seeking his kine there,
And found their track and his, yet hardly cold,
And cried—'What wonder do mine eyes behold!

'Here are the footsteps of the hornèd herd
   Turned back towards their fields of asphodel;—

But *these* are not the tracks of beast or bird,
  Gray wolf, or bear, or lion of the dell,
Or manèd Centaur—sand was never stirred
  By man or woman thus! Inexplicable!
Who with unwearied feet could e'er impress
The sand with such enormous vestiges?

'That was most strange—but this is stranger still!'
  Thus having said, Phoebus impetuously
Sought high Cyllene's forest-cinctured hill,
  And the deep cavern where dark shadows lie,
And where the ambrosial nymph with happy will
  Bore the Saturnian's love-child, Mercury—
And a delightful odour from the dew
Of the hill pastures, at his coming, flew.

And Phoebus stooped under the craggy roof
  Arched over the dark cavern:—Maia's child
Perceived that he came angry, far aloof,
  About the cows of which he had been beguiled;
And over him the fine and fragrant woof
  Of his ambrosial swaddling-clothes he piled—
As among fire-brands lies a burning spark
Covered, beneath the ashes cold and dark.

There, like an infant who had sucked his fill
  And now was newly washed and put to bed,
Awake, but courting sleep with weary will,
  And gathered in a lump, hands, feet, and head,
He lay, and his belovèd tortoise still
  He grasped and held under his shoulder-blade.
Phoebus the lovely mountain-goddess knew,
Not less her subtle, swindling baby, who

Lay swathed in his sly wiles. Round every crook
  Of the ample cavern, for his kine, Apollo
Looked sharp; and when he saw them not, he took
  The glittering key, and opened three great hollow
Recesses in the rock—where many a nook
  Was filled with the sweet food immortals swallow,
And mighty heaps of silver and of gold
Were piled within—a wonder to behold!

And white and silver robes, all overwrought
  With cunning workmanship of tracery sweet—
Except among the Gods there can be nought
  In the wide world to be compared with it.
Latona's offspring, after having sought
  His herds in every corner, thus did greet
Great Hermes:—'Little cradled rogue, declare
Of my illustrious heifers, where they are!

'Speak quickly! or a quarrel between us
  Must rise, and the event will be, that I
Shall hurl you into dismal Tartarus,
  In fiery gloom to dwell eternally;
Nor shall your father nor your mother loose
  The bars of that black dungeon—utterly
You shall be cast out from the light of day,
To rule the ghosts of men, unblessed as they.

To whom thus Hermes slily answered:—'Son
  Of great Latona, what a speech is this!
Why come you here to ask me what is done
  With the wild oxen which it seems you miss?
I have not seen them, nor from any one
  Have heard a word of the whole business;

If you should promise an immense reward,
I could not tell more than you now have heard.

'An ox-stealer should be both tall and strong,
    And I am but a little new-born thing,
Who, yet at least, can think of nothing wrong:—
    My business is to suck, and sleep, and fling
The cradle-clothes about me all day long,—
    Or half asleep, hear my sweet mother sing,
And to be washed in water clean and warm,
And hushed and kissed and kept secure from harm.

'O, let not e'er this quarrel be averred!
    The astounded Gods would laugh at you, if e'er
You should allege a story so absurd
    As that a new born infant forth could fare
Out of his home after a savage herd.
    I was born yesterday—my small feet are
Too tender for the roads so hard and rough:—
And if you think that this is not enough,

'I swear a great oath, by my father's head,
    That I stole not your cows, and that I know
Of no one else, who might, or could, or did.—
    Whatever things cows are, I do not know,
For I have only heard the name.'—This said,
    He winked as fast as could be, and his brow
Was wrinkled, and a whistle loud gave he,
Like one who hears some strange absurdity.

Apollo gently smiled and said:—'Ay, ay,—
    You cunning little rascal, you will bore
Many a rich man's house, and your array
    Of thieves will lay their siege before his door,

123

Silent as night, in night; and many a day
  In the wild glens rough shepherds will deplore
That you or yours, having an appetite,
Met with their cattle, comrade of the night!

'And this among the Gods shall be your gift,
  To be considered as the lord of those
Who swindle, house-break, sheep-steal, and shop-lift;—
  But now if you would not your last sleep doze;
Crawl out!'—Thus saying, Phoebus did uplift
  The subtle infant in his swaddling clothes,
And in his arms, according to his wont,
A scheme devised the illustrious Argiphont.

        .   .   .   .

        .   .   .   .

And sneezed and shuddered—Phoebus on the grass
  Him threw, and whilst all that he had designed
He did perform—eager although to pass,
  Apollo darted from his mighty mind
Towards the subtle babe the following scoff:—
'Do not imagine this will get you off,

'You little swaddled child of Jove and May!'
  And seized him:—'By this omen I shall trace
My noble herds, and you shall lead the way.'—
  Cyllenian Hermes from the grassy place,
Like one in earnest haste to get away,
  Rose, and with hands lifted towards his face
Round both his ears up from his shoulders drew
His swaddling clothes, and—'What mean you to do

'With me, you unkind God?'—said Mercury:
  'Is it about these cows you tease me so?

I wish the race of cows were perished!—I
   Stole not your cows—I do not even know
What things cows are. Alas! I well may sigh
   That, since I came into this world of woe,
I should have ever heard the name of one—
But I appeal to the Saturnian's throne.'

Thus Phoebus and the vagrant Mercury
   Talked without coming to an explanation,
With adverse purpose. As for Phoebus, he
   Sought not revenge, but only information,
And Hermes tried with lies and roguery
   To cheat Apollo.—But when no evasion
Served—for the cunning one his match had found—
He paced on first over the sandy ground.

     .   .   .   .   .

He of the Silver Bow the child of Jove
Followed behind, till to their heavenly Sire
   Came both his children, beautiful as Love,
And from his equal balance did require
   A judgement in the cause wherein they strove.
O'er odorous Olympus and its snows
A murmuring tumult as they came arose,—

And from the folded depths of the great Hill,
   While Hermes and Apollo reverent stood
Before Jove's throne, the indestructible
   Immortals rushed in mighty multitude;
And whilst their seats in order due they fill,
   The lofty Thunderer in a careless mood
To Phoebus said:—'Whence drive you this sweet prey,
This herald-baby, born but yesterday?—

'A most important subject, trifler, this
    To lay before the Gods!'—'Nay, Father, nay,
When you have understood this business,
    Say not that I alone am fond of prey.
I found this little boy in a recess
    Under Cyllene's mountains far away—
A manifest and most apparent thief,
A scandalmonger beyond all belief.

'I never saw his like either in Heaven
    Or upon earth for knavery or craft:—
Out of the field my cattle yester-even,
    By the low shore on which the loud sea laughed,
He right down to the river-ford had driven;
    And mere astonishment would make you daft
To see the double kind of footsteps strange
He has impressed wherever he did range.

'The cattle's track on the black dust, full well
    Is evident, as if they went towards
The place from which they came—that asphodel
    Meadow, in which I feed my many herds,—
His steps were most incomprehensible—
    I know not how I can describe in words
Those tracks—he could have gone along the sands
Neither upon his feet nor on his hands;—

'He must have had some other stranger mode
    Of moving on: those vestiges immense,
Far as I traced them on the sandy road,
    Seemed like the trail of oak-toppings:—but thence
No mark nor track denoting where they trod
    The hard ground gave:—but, working at his fence,

A mortal hedger saw him as he passed
To Pylos, with the cows, in fiery haste.

'I found that in the dark he quietly
    Had sacrificed some cows, and before light
Had thrown the ashes all dispersedly
    About the road—then, still as gloomy night,
Had crept into his cradle, either eye
    Rubbing, and cogitating some new sleight.
No eagle could have seen him as he lay
Hid in his cavern from the peering day.

'I taxed him with the fact, when he averred
    Most solemnly that he did neither see
Nor even had in any manner heard
    Of my lost cows, whatever things cows be;
Nor could he tell, though offered a reward,
    Not even who could tell of them to me.'
So speaking, Phoebus sate; and Hermes then
Addressed the supreme Lord of Gods and Men:—

'Great Father, you know clearly beforehand
    That all which I shall say to you is sooth;
I am a most veracious person, and
    Totally unacquainted with untruth.
At sunrise Phoebus came, but with no band
    Of Gods to bear him witness, in great wrath,
To my abode, seeking his heifers there,
And saying that I must show him where they are,

'Or he would hurl me down the dark abyss.
    I know that every Apollonian limb
Is clothed with speed and might and manliness,
    As a green bank with flowers—but unlike him

127

I was born yesterday, and you may guess
    He well knew this when he indulged the whim
Of bullying a poor little new-born thing
That slept, and never thought of cow-driving.

'Am I like a strong fellow who steals kine?
    Believe me, dearest Father—such you are—
This driving of the herds is none of mine;
    Across my threshold did I wander ne'er,
So may I thrive! I reverence the divine
    Sun and the Gods, and I love you, and care
Even for this hard accuser—who must know
I am as innocent as they or you.

'I swear by these most gloriously-wrought portals
    (It is, you will allow, an oath of might)
Through which the multitude of the Immortals
    Pass and repass forever, day and night,
Devising schemes for the affairs of mortals—
    That I am guiltless; and I will requite,
Although mine enemy be great and strong,
His cruel threat—do thou defend the young!'

So speaking, the Cylenian Argiphont
    Winked, as if now his adversary was fitted:—
And Jupiter, according to his wont,
    Laughed heartily to hear the subtle-witted
Infant give such a plausible account,
    And every word a lie. But he remitted
Judgement at present—and his exhortation
Was, to compose the affair by arbitration.

Matilda Gathering Flowers

FROM THE PURGATORIO OF DANTE,
CANTO XXVIII, ll. 1–51

And earnest to explore within—around—
  The divine wood, whose thick green living woof
  Tempered the young day to the sight—I wound
Up the green slope, beneath the forest's roof,
  With slow, soft steps leaving the mountain's steep,
  And sought those inmost labyrinths, motion-proof
Against the air, that in that stillness deep
  And solemn, struck upon my forehead bare,
  The slow, soft stroke of a continuous . . .
In which the   leaves tremblingly were
  All bent towards that part where earliest
  The sacred hill obscures the morning air.
Yet were they not so shaken from the rest,
  But that the birds, perched on the utmost spray,
  Incessantly renewing their blithe quest,
With perfect joy received the early day,
  Singing within the glancing leaves, whose sound
  Kept a low burden to their roundelay,
Such as from bough to bough gathers around
  The pine forest on bleak Chiassi's shore,
  When Aeolus Sirocco has unbound.
My slow steps had already borne me o'er
  Such space within the antique wood, that I
  Perceived not where I entered any more,—

When, lo! a stream whose little waves went by,
    Bending towards the left through grass that grew
    Upon its bank, impeded suddenly
My going on. Water of purest hue
    On earth, would appear turbid and impure
    Compared with this, whose unconcealing dew,
Dark, dark, yet clear, moved under the obscure
    Eternal shades, whose interwoven looms
    The rays of moon or sunlight ne'er endure.
I moved not with my feet, but mid the glooms
    Pierced with my charmèd eye, contemplating
    The mighty multitude of fresh May blooms
Which starred that night, when, even as a thing
    That suddenly, for blank astonishment,
    Charms every sense, and makes all thought take wing,—
A solitary woman! and she went
    Singing and gathering flower after flower,
    With which her way was painted and besprent.
'Bright lady, who, if looks had ever power
    To bear true witness of the heart within,
    Dost bask under the beams of love, come lower
Towards this bank. I prithee let me win
    This much of thee, to come, that I may hear
    Thy song: like Prosperine, in Enna's glen,
Thou seemest to my fancy, singing here
    And gathering flowers, as that fair maiden when
    She lost the Spring, and Ceres her, more dear.'

PROSE EXTRACTS

(i) *The Beauty of the God of Love (from Shelley's translation of Plato's Symposium, 195–6)*

There were need of some poet like Homer to celebrate the delicacy and tenderness of Love. For Homer says, that the goddess Calamity is delicate, and that her feet are tender. 'Her feet are soft,' he says, 'for she treads not upon the ground, but makes her path upon the heads of men'. He gives as evidence of her tenderness, that she walks not upon that which is hard, but that which is soft. The same evidence is sufficient to make manifest the tenderness of Love. For Love walks not upon the earth, nor over the heads of men, which are not indeed very soft; but he dwells within, and treads on the softest of existing things, having established his habitation within the souls and inmost nature of Gods and men;—not indeed in all souls—for wherever he chances to find a hard and rugged disposition, there he will not inhabit, but only where it is most soft and tender. Of needs must he be the most delicate of all things, who touches lightly with his feet, only the softest parts of those things which are the softest of all.

He is then the youngest and the most delicate of all divinities; and in addition to this, he is, as it were, the most moist and liquid. For if he were otherwise, he could not, as he does, fold himself around everything, and secretly flow out and into every soul. His loveliness, that which Love possesses beyond all other things, is a manifestation of the liquid and flowing symmetry of his form; for between deformity and Love there is eternal contrast and repugnance. His life is spent among flowers, and this accounts for the immortal fairness of his skin; for the winged Love rests not in his flight on any form, or within any soul the flower of whose loveliness is faded, but there remains most willingly where is the odour and radiance of blossoms, yet unwithered. Concerning the beauty of the God, let this be sufficient, though many things must remain unsaid.

(ii) *Love as Creator and Harmonizer Everywhere* (Symposium, 197)

And who will deny that the divine poetry, by which all living things are produced upon the earth, is not harmonized by the wisdom of Love? Is it not evident that Love was the author of all the arts of life with which we are acquainted, and that he whose teacher has been Love, becomes eminent and illustrious, whilst he who knows not Love, remains forever unregarded and obscure? Apollo invented medicine, and divination, and archery, under the guidance of desire and Love; so that Apollo was the disciple of Love. Through him the Muses discovered the arts of literature, and Vulcan that of moulding brass, and Minerva the loom, and Jupiter the mystery of the dominion which he now exercises over Gods and men. So were the Gods taught and disciplined by the love of that which is beautiful; for there is no love towards deformity.

At the origin of things, as I have before said, many fearful deeds were reported to have been done among the Gods on account of the dominion of Necessity. But so soon as this deity sprang forth from the desire which forever tends in the universe towards that which is lovely, then all blessings descended upon all living things, human and divine. Love seems to me, O Phaedrus, a divinity the most beautiful and the best of all, and the author to all others of the excellences with which his own nature is endowed. Nor can I restrain the poetic enthusiasm which takes possession of my discourse, and bids me declare that Love is the divinity who creates peace among men, and calm upon the sea, the windless silence of storms, repose and sleep in sadness. Love divests us of all alienation from each other, and fills our vacant hearts with overflowing sympathy; he gathers us together in such social meetings as we now delight to celebrate, our guardian and our guide in dances, and sacrifices, and feasts. Yes, Love who showers benignity upon the world, and before whose presence all harsh passions flee and perish; the author of all soft affections; the destroyer of all ungentle thoughts; merciful, mild; the object of the admiration of the wise, and the delight of gods; possessed by the fortunate, and desired by the unhappy, therefore unhappy because they possess him not; the father of grace, and delicacy, and gentleness, and delight, and persuasion, and desire; the cherisher of all that is good, the abolisher of all evil; our most excellent pilot, defence, saviour and guardian in labour and in fear, in desire and in reason; the ornament and governor of all things human and divine; the best, the loveliest; in whose footsteps everyone ought to follow, celebrating him excellently in song, and bearing each his part in that divinest harmony which Love sings to all things which live and are, soothing the troubled minds of Gods and men. This, O Phaedrus, is what I have to offer in praise of the divinity; partly composed, indeed, of thoughtless and playful fancies, and partly of such serious ones, as I could well command.

NOTES

THE BOAT ON THE SERCHIO

Written at Pisa on the Serchio, summer 1821. Probably uncompleted.

36. Lionel is Shelley, Melchior is Edward Williams (see *Summary*).

67. *Della Cruscan:* a member of the 16th-century Florentine Academy founded to purify the Italian language.

80. Shelley and Williams were both schoolboys at Eton.

5. LETTER TO MARIA GISBORNE

Introduction p. xxi; *Summary* p. xxxviii.

59. *swink:* toil (archaic).

75. *idealism:* design, plan.

114. *Libeccio:* the south-west wind.

127. *eye of Love:* a small patch of blue sky.

181. *Calderon:* (1600–81), a Spanish comic dramatist, whom Shelley admired and translated.

213. *Shout:* a popular London print-seller (Leigh Hunt's study is also described in some detail in Keats's poem *Sleep and Poetry*, ll. 350 ff).

219. *and there is he:* possibly Charles Lamb.

273. Henry Reveley (see *Summary*, p. xxxviii).

274. *I see:* contrast l. 257.

302 ff. Shelley's well-known abstemious diet.

15. THE AZIOLA

9. *mockery of myself:* a human being enough like himself to remind him of his own shortcomings. Shelley is either using 'elate' to mean 'eager', or (more likely) the sentence in ll. 7–12 inverts the sequence of events.

11. *disquiet:* a trisyllable.

16. SONNET: ENGLAND IN 1819

The references are to George III, the feeble 'Royal Dukes', the Liverpool Ministry, the 'Peterloo Massacre', the government use of *agent provocateurs*, and the House of Commons (unreformed until 1832).

18. THE MASK OF ANARCHY

This poem, easily the best of Shelley's political verse, was written in response to the 'Peterloo Massacre' which occurred near Manchester, 16th August 1819. The poem opens with a 'Triumph' of Anarchy (whose followers are likened to members of the Liverpool Ministry) with despairing Hope throwing herself before Anarchy's chariot as if it were a Juggernaut. At that moment, however, the scene is interrupted by the apparition of a great Angel of Love. Hope reappears, and the rest of the poem is 'as if' (l. 139) Earth were speaking to men her children. Shelley portrays his angel as a Satanic one (since his poem opens with the forces of evil on earth worshipping a god of evil, like Jupiter in *Prometheus Unbound*) and his treatment owes something to Milton's account of the transformations of Satan (*Paradise Lost*, IV, 810 ff; X. 447–50). More clearly, however, Shelley has combined details from Dante's account of seeing the first angel, and of seeing Mars glowing red, in *Purgatorio* II, 13–39.

22–3.   the Bible's black binding and white paper.

112.   *grain:* (iridescent) crimson: see the next line.

119.   See Appendix B, passage (i) ll. 4–5.

145.   *accent:* in the sense of utterance.

220.   *Fame:* in the old sense of *Rumour*.

233.   *That:* = what.

308.   *startling:* see *Introduction*, p. xvi.

364–5.   shall steam up *to the nation:* 'steam' in its older sense of 'be exhaled' (cf. *Comus*, l. 556, 'a steam of rich distill'd perfumes').

31. PETER BELL THE THIRD, PART THE FIFTH

Written at Florence in October 1819, a burlesque of Wordsworth's naive but supernatural ballad *Peter Bell*. *Peter Bell the First* was in fact a skit published (in April 1819) a few days *in advance* of its original, Wordsworth's poem. It was written by Keats's friend John Hamilton

135

Reynolds, who had got wind of what Wordsworth was bringing out. In the extract now printed, Peter (= Wordsworth) is in Hell, and a footman to the Devil. The 'man . . . fair as a maid' is Coleridge. There is much insight and sympathy in the poem, as well as burlesque.

34. HELLAS: THE FINAL CHORUS

Summary, p. xxxix.

3-4. Spring gives the world a new bright covering that comes up under the dark covering of winter like a snake's new skin breaking through the old one (*Introduction*, pp. xxiii-xxiv).

6. *wrecks:* remnants, ruins.

31. The Golden Age of the future will come when Saturn, once ousted by Jove, resumes his reign.

33-34. A note by Shelley indicates that these lines refer to (i) the Gods of Greece, Asia, and Egypt, reputed in legend to have fallen at the coming of (ii) Christ; and (iii) the still surviving idolatries of China, India, etc.

37. *Cease:* the chorus is as if telling itself to say no more, as the rest may be unhappy.

36. OZYMANDIAS

First printed (in Hunt's *Examiner*) January 1818.

6-8. The king's passions, seen by the sculptor and expressed by him in the stone, survive the sculptor's silently ironical carving ('hand that mocked'), and the king himself ('heart that fed'). The irony transpires when the true cause for the 'despair' in l. 11 is seen.

36. RARELY, RARELY   1821

Introduction, p. xiii. The point of the earlier stanzas is that those who are already happy get more happiness, while unhappy people seem to be left unhappy.

38-39 THE INDIAN SERENADE and TO SOPHIA

The first of these poems was inspired by the aria 'Ah perdona' in Mozart's *La Clemenza di Tito*, and presented by Shelley to Sophia Stacey, a ward of one of his uncles, when she visited Florence during

November 1819. It was published in Leigh Hunt's *Liberal* (1822) as a *Song Written for an Indian Air*. Since Miss Stacey 'played the harp, and sang very sweetly' (E. Blunden, *Shelley*, 1948 ed., p. 213), the serenade is best taken as written for singing by a woman. There is an interesting contrast in tone and style between it and *To Sophia*, where Shelley writes in his own person and for the speaking voice.

40. I FEAR THY KISSES

Originally dated 1820, but probably also written for Sophia Stacey.

40. TO JANE: 'THE KEEN STARS . . .'

Written in 1822 and first published (by Medwin) as *An Ariette for Music, To a Lady singing to her Accompaniment on the Guitar*. The lady is Jane Williams (*Summary*, p. xxxix).

6. *again:* the singer repeated the melody first played by the guitar.

STANZAS 2 and 3: The singer dominates her instrument as the moon does the starry sky; but (presumably the singing is *al fresco*) in respect of her surroundings as a whole, she is more dominant still.

41. 'ONE WORD IS TOO OFTEN PROFANED' 1821

Addressed to Jane Williams, or possibly to Emilia Viviani, a young Italian girl whom Shelley deeply admired for some time after he met her in December 1820.

8. *that:* hope (l. 5).

9. the stress is on 'men': physical as opposed to spiritual love.

42. AN EXHORTATION 1819

A witty piece developed from Sidney's phrase, 'the chameleon poet', in his *Apology*; but it also has a kind of exhilarated poignancy typical of Shelley.

19. *Yet:* the contrast intended is between poets' proper rewards (love, fame: which, however, they fail to get), and wealth or power which are useless substitutes.

22. chameleons live up in trees, lizards crawl on the ground.

Summary, p. xxxviii. Shelley's taking the skylark singing in the sky to represent a spiritual power that can spread its influence through the world is reminiscent of Plato, *Phaedrus* 246, 249, where the soul is seen as growing real wings and mounting aloft on them. (Shelley is said to have translated this work, but the translation has been lost).

8. *cloud of fire:* the point is that this bursts up and then, like the skylark, vanishes (cf. 'unbodied' l. 15); here is also the point of the series of comparisons in ll. 36–56: the lark is singing too high up in the air to be seen.

22–3. . . . *intense lamp narrows* . . . T. S. Eliot quotes this in illustration of Shelley's confusion in writing, without realizing that it describes (and aptly) Venus; not the moon, to which Shelley refers in the next stanza.

64–5. *Praise of love:* the phrase should be taken with, say, the banquet speeches in Plato's *Symposium* in mind.

82–5. . . . *of death must deem:* the skylark's song flows happily because death is no mystery and therefore no terror to it.

88–9. *sincerest . . . some:* the sense requires these words to be stressed.

103. *madness:* poetic inspiration (cf. Plato's *Ion*).

47. THE QUESTION

Written in 1820.

10–11. *Arcturi:* like Arcturus, a star which is a bright white colour (daisies remain open all night).

15. *mother:* the earth.

20. the sense is presumably 'not yet drained . . .'

36–8. the 'imprisoned children . . .' (the flowers) kept the like array.

40. the meaning is unexpectedly uncertain. N. I. White (*Shelley*, Vol. II, p. 563) takes the line as expressing 'despair of finding a recipient' for the flowers. If however we accept his other suggestion (*ibid.*, p. 190) that the poem may have been written in December 1819 (the poet is speaking in winter and dreaming of spring), then the poem is easily seen as a compliment addressed to Sophia Stacey, and the last line as meaning that only one recipient is conceivable, not that there is none.

Introduction, pp. xiv, xv; *Summary*, p. xxxvii. See also *Letter to Maria Gisborne* l. 115—the South-West wind bringing thunder—and ll. 150 ff.

Part of Shelley's own note reads, 'This poem was conceived and chiefl˙ written in a wood that skirts the Arno, near Florence, and on a day when that tempestuous wind, whose temperature is at once mild and animating, was collecting the vapours which pour down the autumn-al rains. They began, as I foresaw, at sunset with a violent tempest of hail and rain, attended by that magnificent thunder and lightning peculiar to the Cisalpine regions'.

The much-discussed second stanza deals with a distinctive and spec-tacular event which the poet has observed with great fullness and accuracy. A large 'anvil' thunderstorm cloud is mounting in the western sky ('steep sky', l. 15, rightly suggests that such a cloud seems to rise vertically). The wind is high, and the two arms of the anvil are fraying out forwards into long, fibrous cirrus clouds like the hair of a Maenad blown forward from her head by the wind (l. 21). The base of the anvil is dissolving in streams of small clouds ('found at the base, or even more often on the lower surface, of anvil projections', H. Duncan Grant, *Cloud and Weather Atlas*, p. 84). Finally, the sun ('this closing night' l. 24) is setting in the west, and the whole cloud is thus partly in deep shadow, partly a rich ruddy colour. Here, in fact, is the crucial point of the whole passage. Coloured in this way, the storm-cloud looks like a gigantic tree, with the loose, flying lower clouds streaming from it like autumn leaves (l. 16) and the upper, cirrus clouds looking like its branches (l. 17: 'of Heaven and Ocean' is in the sense of 'made from Heaven and Ocean, air, and water-vapour').

The storm-cloud, likened to a holy sepulchre with a religious fire, is implicit in the 'incantation', the 'prophecy', and the sparks from the 'unextinguished hearth', of the last stanza; which also reverts to the contrast between winter and spring in the first, and suggests a likeness between the clarion of the new year and the trumpet-note of true poetry.

The closing lines of stanza IV are best seen as the traditional cry of the poet-prophet calling for inspiration to sustain him in a decaying and hostile world. (Cf. F. A. Pottle, *The Case of Shelley*, Proceedings of the Modern Language Association, 1952, p. 589; and *Psalms* 18, 4–6, or *Isaiah* 21, 3–4.)

Shelley's note on ll. 37–41 reads, 'The phenomenon alluded to at the conclusion of the third stanza is well known to naturalists. The vegetation at the bottom of the sea, of rivers, and of lakes, sympathizes with that of the land in the change of seasons, and is consequently influenced by the winds which announce it'.

The metre of the poem is unusual: a 14-line stanza constructed from five *terza rima* terzine, with the penultimate line omitted and the stanza thus ended in a couplet.

17–21. it is the 'tangled boughs' that resemble angels and what follows the colon (l. 18) says why: 'the locks of the approaching storm' (l. 23) resemble the hair of a Maenad (l. 21). An early draft (*Shelley Notebooks*, ed. H. Buxton Forman, 1911, p. 163) sets this beyond doubt, but it seems also the best reading of the text itself.

43–5. the leaf, cloud and wave resume stanzas I–III.

51. HYMN OF APOLLO   1820

Apollo is seen in his traditional roles as Sun-god (from night through day to evening) and god of intellectual light, poetry, the arts, and medicine.

52. THE CLOUD

Summary, p. xxxviii.

Shelley may have derived some of the scientific ideas in this poem from Father Giovanni Battista Beccaria's treatise on *Artificial Electricity*; but more probably from lectures by Adam Walker (see *Introduction*). The verse form may come from street-ballads (see V. da Sola Pinto and A. E. Rodway, *The Common Muse*, p. 26).

The poem seems wild and confused at first, but really combines great animation with much insight and accuracy. Nevertheless, it well illustrates the general points made in the *Introduction* (p. xxxi).

7–8. *their mother:* the earth. The flowers are closing at night. (But 'birds' is an alternative reading for 'buds' l. 6.)

11. *it:* the hail that had already fallen (l. 9).

15–16. the stationary cloud forms and dissolves continuously over the summit.

22. for the contemporary idea that local air currents among clouds are caused by lightning, see *Introduction*, p. xx.

31. *meteor eyes:* glaring 'gaze' like a meteor?

38. the Eagle is imagined as lit by its own golden light: hence the sun is like it.

53. *whirl and flee:* an optical illusion; the stars appear to move rather than the cloud passing over them. Cf. Wordsworth, *Excursion*, IV. 869–71:

> ' . . . moon and stars
> Glance rapidly along the clouded heaven
> When winds are blowing strong.'

55. *my wind built tent:* the cloud *is* the tent.

58. *these:* the stars.

79. *convex gleams:* following the curvature of the earth; another idea which Shelley seems to have derived from the science of his day.

81. *cenotaph:* the clear sky is cenotaph of the cloud, and 'unbuilt' as the cloud re-forms.

82. *the caverns of rain:* the 'blue dome', transformed by rain-bearing storm-clouds, is now seen as a cavern.

55. ODE TO HEAVEN

Dated 'Florence, December 1819'. The three Spirits describe, in turn, something like the sky of the astronomer, Heaven in comparatively orthodox religious terms, and the Platonic Intelligible World to which the world of sense is a transient appendage.

57. ADONAIS

For the date of this poem, and for Shelley's acquaintance with and admiration of Keats, see *Summary*, p. xxxviii. The central movement of thought in the poem is from an awareness of spring's renewing the earth again, although the most genuinely creative of human artists is dead, to a conviction that this paradox is a fiction, because for an immortal poet there can be no such thing as death. Shelley sees this as true not only in the immortality of fame, but even more because bodily death gives the poet fuller life by re-uniting him with the spiritual principle transfusing the whole world: the originating source of beauty, of which poets are therefore the truest servants.

Adonis, the god who experiences rebirth through death at the hands of his persecutors, stood well for a poet whom Shelley (mistakenly) supposed to have been brought to his death through savage attacks by reviewers. Shelley had translated part of the Greek poet Bion's *Lament for Adonis*, and his poem owes to this one not only something of its melodious elegaic tone, but also its title (a Doric form of Adonis); its opening conception of the mourning loves and echoes; the lamenting procession to Adonais's tomb; the grief of Urania (Cytherea in Bion's poem); and the transforming idea that the dead poet finds rebirth as part of the life of nature. Most of these, however, had long been a part of the tradition of formal elegy.

Shelley is thus right in describing his poem as 'a highly wrought *piece of art*'; but he leads it on from its leisurely and elaborately decorous opening stanzas, through the tributes to Byron, Moore, and Leigh Hunt, and the record (its weakest part) of his own loneliness and persecution, to a noble expression of his deepest convictions about the greatness of true poetry and the existence of a spiritual reality which both redeems and transcends the world of sense.

4. *Hour:* in the Greek sense, one of the spirits of the seasons.

12. *Urania:* The Muse of astronomy, and of all solemn and ambitious poetry.

15. *one:* one 'Echo' entranced Urania by uttering Keats's poems.

29. *He:* Milton (following Homer and Dante).

149. *with morning:* the mother eagle is said to teach her eaglets to gaze directly at the sun.

250. *Pythian:* Byron (likened to Apollo); the reference is to his satirical *English Bards and Scotch Reviewers*.

268-9. Thomas Moore.

271-306. In these stanzas Shelley, thinking of his own isolation and misfortunes, is likening himself to both the god Dionysus (Greek equivalent of Adonis: his chariot was drawn by 'pards', leopards); and to the Wandering Jew.

312. Leigh Hunt.

347-8. Cf. *Hamlet*, II. 2., the First Player representing Pyrrhus at the sack of Troy.

379–87. A platonic idea: things in the world of matter tend to revert to their original nature in the World of Forms.

381. *plastic:* creative.

411. In the Ptolemaic astronomy, each of the heavenly spheres is governed by a celestial being called an 'intelligence'.

415–23. the point is that a human spirit (that equally of Adonais, or the mourner) can pervade the whole universe, or concentrate at a minute point, because it is essentially not material.

440. Shelley's son William was also buried (June 1819) in the Protestant cemetery at Rome.

444–6. *one keen pyramid:* this is the tomb of Caius Cestius, a 1st century A.D. Roman.

73. THE WITCH OF ATLAS

Completed in three days, 14–16th August 1820, at the Baths of San Guiliano near Pisa. The 'Witch' is no witch in the traditional English sense, but a spirit, the daughter of a sea-nymph, who incarnates the beauty and love that pervades the world, and who descends by stages from her private paradise (a cave-and-bower which has many distinctive details in common with Porphyry's *Cave of the Nymphs*) to contemplate and disturb the ugly and un-lovely doings of man. She may owe her origin to a passage in Vergil (*Aeneid* IV, 480–93) which describes a priestess of Atlas (father of the sea-nymphs) who had similar powers, and whose retreat was also in Ethiopia (Shelley had finished Book IV of the *Aeneid* the previous April). Her consort Hermaphroditus may derive in part from ideas of the bisexual nature of love in the *Symposium*, or from Spenser's regularly thinking of the spirit of nature as hermaphrodite, or from Ovid's story of the love of Salmacis and Hermaphroditus, both descendants of Atlas (*Metamorphoses* IV, 285–388). Most important, the Witch is fairly clearly a kind of counterpart to Hermes in the Homeric *Hymn to Mercury*, which Shelley had translated into verse only a few weeks before he wrote this poem, and the two works have something of the same very distinctive tone, imaginative and meaningful yet shifting and whimsical. Shelley was also by now acquainted with, in this respect, similar works by Byron, like *Beppo* and the early cantos of *Don Juan*, and with their Italian sources. (Keats's *The Cap and Bells* is relevant to this aspect of English Romantic poetry.)

With all these (save the last) more or less in mind, Shelley has nevertheless created a highly original work with a striking quality of lightness and spontaneity.

The passage selected is not perhaps the most remarkable in the poem, but it illustrates most clearly the abrupt though deft and unobtrusive transitions of tone which are so distinctive of it.

75. Extracts from PROMETHEUS UNBOUND

Summary, p. xxxvii; *Introduction*, pp. xxv, xxix.

Some general note of this important work seems justified. *Prometheus Unbound* is undramatic and sometimes awkward in its dialogue, but it centres upon a strikingly dramatic action. This comprises two parallel transformations: the release of Prometheus, on account of his abiding mercifulness, at what looks like the very moment of his greatest suffering and humiliation from the evil spirits who minister to Jupiter the tyrant (Act I, 632 ff); and the casting down of Jupiter by the World-Spirit Demogorgon (Destiny) at the very moment of his extremest arrogance and self-glorification (Act III. Sc. 1, 51 ff). Act II depicts the descent of Asia and Panthea (daughters of Ocean and spirits of love) from Earth to the cave of Demogorgon, where they see the 'Hour' of Jupiter's downfall issuing from the cave of Fate and rising to the upper world to carry out its mission. Act III, after that downfall has occurred, depicts the emancipation of Prometheus as the great patron and protector of mankind, and the regeneration of human life which follows.

The first three acts were written between October 1818 and April 1819. Act IV (completed in December 1819) envisages an ensuing regeneration (ll. 156–7 afford the key) of the whole cosmos, celebrated through a culminating series of lyrics or lyrical speeches uttered first by the spirits who preside over it, and then by Demogorgon himself. In this poem, Shelley sees the coming of the millenium as a deep spiritual change in men themselves; and the speech of Demogorgon at the close of Act IV makes especially clear his measured and indeed sombre conception of the possible future of mankind.

The passages selected here are:

(i) a lyrical chorus from Act II. Scene ii, depicting part of the descent of the spirits of Love, Asia, and Panthea, to Demogorgon's cave.

(ii) a lyric from Act II. Scene v, celebrating the miraculous transformation of Asia at the moment when Prometheus's release and the regeneration of the world are imminent.

(iii) the whole of Act IV.

The strength of *Prometheus Unbound* as a whole lies in its visionary power and insight (both words bear weighing), and also in its frequently rich, intricate robustness of language and thought (see the first lyric included), combined as this is with astonishing and sustained rhythmical virtuosity and music. It is essentially a lyrical drama: the action of the play may be dramatic in its ironical contrasts, but it is very much not so in its arbitrariness. The main events succeed each other as the events of a pageant, for their significance not their inevitability. The 'necessity' which they are meant to illustrate is something not to be felt in the action. More serious, some of the detailed handling fails to satisfy. Shelley personalizes cosmic love in a manner which comes too close to the 18th-century cult of sensibility; another aspect of which (like his excessive admiration for Guido Reni) shows in the overstrained section (Act I, 580–630) when Prometheus is tortured by being shown a vision of Christ on the Cross.

(i) '*The path through which that lovely twain . . .*'

The syntax of this beautiful lyric is condensed but not confused. The following is a skeleton, with one word which needs to be understood inserted in italics:

> 'The path . . . is curtained out . . .; Nor sun, nor moon . . . can pierce its . . . bowers . . . save where some cloud of dew . . . hangs . . . a pearl . . . and (one frail . . . anemone) bends and then fades silently, or *save* when some star . . . has found the cleft . . .' The 'it' of what follows 'those depths upon' is the star: imagine a colon after 'upon'.

(ii) '*Life of Life! thy lips enkindle . . .*'

9–10. the morning sunlight suffuses through the clouds before its heat dispels them.

16. *splendour:* radiance (cf. *Adonais* l. 363; *Mask of Anarchy* l. 135).

21. *of whom:* of those whom.

(iii) *Act IV*

81. Panthea and Ione (the third sea-nymph) speak in blank verse throughout the Act.

185. *awful:* awe-inspiring. (See *Introduction*, p. xix.)

186–8.   the 'music of the spheres' (cf. Plato, *Republic*, 617).

206 ff.   Ione and Panthea see a vision of two spirits, representing the Moon (l. 206) and the Earth.

254.   *bright brook:* (?) the 'ocean-like enchantment' of music (l. 203) within which the whole scene is set. But this is obscure.

269.   *mocking:* imitating (as happy speech imitates music).

270 ff.   the light from the stars upon the forehead of the spirit of Earth transfuses the whole sphere of the earth (as this advances in the vision) and displays its past history as laid down age by age on its surface. (Cf. a very similar though less comprehensive passage in Keats, *Endymion* III, l. 119 et seq. Volney, *Ruins of Empires,* is perhaps the influential primary source.)

338 ff.   the construction is, 'Sceptred curse . . . how art thou sunk . . .' (l. 350).

374.   the construction is 'It (the spirit of reawakening love in the world) wakes a life . . . . . . till hate, and fear . . . fleeing, leave Man, who was a many-sided mirror . . . a sea reflecting love (love which over all his kind . . . doth move) . . . (and leave) Man . . . a chain of linked thought . . . (and) one harmonious soul (made from) many a soul (etc.)'.

429.   *less mighty:* life, once it starts on the moon, will produce a pro-portionately smaller race of beings.

474.   *Agave:* a maenad worshipper of Dionysus. This also explains 'maniac-like', l. 470.

519.   *happy soul:* that of earth itself.

523.   before the voice of the all-powerful ruling spirit of the world.

554.   *which down:* this day gapes open, across the whole cosmos from Hell to Heaven, to capture the tyrant Jupiter. In this closing lyric the train of thought is firm and controlled. First there is this open abyss, then Conquest is dragged deep into it; the spirit of love springs up above; Gentleness, Virtue, etc., seal the chasm over the evil spirit (now seen as the Serpent in the pit); and if that serpent should ever start to escape (as in time is possible), the closing stanza prescribes what to do.

100.   THE TRIUMPH OF LIFE

Introduction, pp. xxv–vi; *Summary,* p. xxxix. The meaning of this diffi-cult and intricate poem is better brought out by a detailed commentary than by a general preliminary note. The work breaks off at l. 544, and has also a number of minor gaps, because Shelley left it unfinished at his death. This poem is usually printed in *terza rima* triads, elaborately punctuated with inverted commas to mark the direct speech. I have taken the liberty here of printing it in verse paragraphs, which makes for a much simpler punctuation, and also helps the reader to grasp the narrative more easily. One should not allow this typographical arrangement to obscure the interlocking rhymes which are sustained throughout the poem, and make its movement utterly different from blank verse.

33–9. the poet seems to sense that he has passed through just this moment once before in a previous life; and the idea serves as an introduction to the central conception of the poem, which is that the 'Life' which enjoys the Triumph is life only in Plato's sense of life in the world of mortality (cf. l. 131, and Plato, *Meno*, 86 or *Phaedrus*, 251).

79 ff. The advancing chariot, glittering with harsh white light and making the sun dim, has in it a bent, dark figure, and seems like the new moon with the old moon cradled in its crescent.

99. *four faces:* cf. the apocalyptic chariot in *Ezekiel* I. 6.

120 ff. those who succeed and those who fail are both in different senses the victims of Life, and parade in its Triumph as prisoners.

131. *native noon:* the heavenly world.

162. Shelley has turned the Triumphal procession into something like a Juggernaut scene (probably following Southey's *Curse of Kehama*, XIV. 4 ff.).

168. *seeking:* the 1824 *Posthumous Poems* has 'limping'.

191. *scorn:* shame, disgrace.

236. these are all eighteenth-century autocratic monarchs.

252. *how:* H. Buxton Forman (*The Poetical Works of Shelley*, 1892) suggests *now* as an emendation.

256. Even Plato, Shelley implies, fell into the power of Life through his infatuation for the boy Aster (Greek for a star).

261. Aristotle, Alexander the Great.

274–81. The ancient poets ruled over their own passions, and their words evoke passions already latent in the reader; Rousseau's writings express his own unmastered sufferings and thus can bring suffering

more in the way of deeds than mere words—though not the deeds of tyrants like (l. 284) the Roman Emperors.

288. *Gregory and John:* popes.

290. *eclipse:* the papal power.

308. *prime:* spring.

313. *cavern:* this cavern, which is at the same time a grove of trees and a fountain, is like that discussed in Porphyry's *The Cave of the Nymphs,* from which human souls are born into the world, and in being born forget everything of their previous and happier existence (see, e.g., W. B. Yeats, 'The Philosophy of Shelley's Poetry', in *Ideas of Good and Evil,* p. 64; the account of the cave on which Porphyry's essay was a commentary comes in the *Odyssey* XIII, 103–112).

325. *his:* the sun's. King and mother both forget their losses the same evening.

346. *well:* the source.

357. *scarf:* leaving iridescent dew. (The passage may be adapted from *Purgatorio,* XXIX. 73–8.)

358. *her:* this is the 'Shape all Light' (not Iris), the nymph of the cave, whose 'crystal glass' is filled with the waters of forgetfulness from the spring (see ll. 359, 382–4, and the reference to the 'light of Heaven', l. 429).

372–3. *Or:* this should probably read 'moist amethyst *Of* the faint morning beams'. This whole scene runs parallel to, but contrasts with, the closing cantos of Dante's *Purgatorio.* There Dante, passing from a lower world to a higher one, passes from the mountain into a grove (in fact, Eden) through which runs a rivulet. Here he meets the lady Matilda singing and picking flowers, whom he sees as like Proserpine, and who in the end baptizes him in the waters of Lethe. But for Dante, this brings oblivion of the lower world as a prelude to a vision of Heaven. The direction of the change and nature of the oblivion is for Rousseau of course the opposite of that. (Shelley's ll. 314–16 follow *Purgatorio* XXVIII, 25–7; his ll. 355–6, *Purgatorio* XXX, 75–8; and his l. 357, *Purgatorio* XXIX, 73–5).

405–11. The first vision (of the 'Shape all Light') corresponds to the footprints of the deer. This is erased by the nepenthean draught (the first wave), and is followed by the second vision (which the poem is about to narrate) corresponding to the footprints of the wolf. The words 'until the second burst' have great significance. What was to succeed the 'new vision', and prove its transience also, would have clearly transpired only if Shelley had completed his poem. There is a suggestion, however, in the lines which follow these. The beautiful 'Shape all Light' survives within the 'harsh glare' of day just as the morning star (Lucifer, l. 414) is present, though invisible because of the sunlight, all day in the sky. Moreover, Shelley adds that the presence of the star is felt all the time by one who wishes to end the day as he began it: viz., 'in that star's smile' (ll. 417-9; cf. also 'Follow it thou even to the night', l. 195). Since Lucifer. the morning star, *is* Venus, the spirit of love both human and divine, the conclusion of the poem and thus its whole organization may perhaps be inferred. The brutal 'Triumph of Life' of the opening pages was to be supplanted by a 'Triumph of Love' in which Rousseau would follow (through a second Nepenthe, to the heavenly world) something like the upward path of Dante or of Adonais ('He hath awakened from the dream of life'). The device of the triumph of one Triumph over another is that on which Petrarch based his *Trionfi* (which Shelley had recently been studying) and was of course a Renaissance commonplace. Petrarch also expresses, throughout the *Trionfi*, an attitude towards life which seems to blend Platonism and ascetic Christian tradition, and is not unlike that in Shelley's poem. Dante, however, is a more significant and intimate influence; and a triumph of spiritual love which puts the sun to shame comes in *Purgatorio* XXIX, 106 ff.

444-5. *forbade/Shadow to fall:* the radiance came from all sides, and so there were no shadows.

464. *early:* Forman suggests 'aery'; but 'early' makes good sense.

465. *upon its motion:* that of the stream.

472. *him:* Dante.

485. *ere evening:* another hint, perhaps, that the poem was to end with the coming of evening, and the reappearance of Venus, the morning and also evening star. All three *cantichë* of the *Divine Comedy* close with the reappearance of the stars of heaven.

487. *phantoms:* these are the thoughts (notably of the kinds indicated in ll. 508-510) which issue from men, and as they do so, age men and wear them out.

539. *oblivious:* having forgotten the heaven from which they came.

543. *abide:* understand 'and (with whom) least . . .', balancing 'from whose forms', l. 542.

544. The closing line may well be an ejaculation by the poet in answer to Rousseau: its point is the paradox that it is life itself which is bringing about the universal atrophy.

INDEX OF FIRST LINES

INDEX OF TITLES